She's Not Just Angry - She's Growing

UNDERSTANDING TEEN GIRL EMOTIONS....

By Ritu Kharb

About the Book

"She's Not Just Angry — She's Growing" is not just another parenting manual. It's a heartfelt invitation to see beyond the storm of teenage emotions and into the heart of a girl who is trying—quietly, clumsily and courageously—to become herself. Set against the familiar rhythms of Indian family life but echoing universally across cultures and homes, this book gently unpacks the emotional complexities of raising a daughter through her pre-teen and adolescent years. In a world where girls are growing up faster than ever—bombarded by social pressures, body image expectations, academic demands and a whirlwind of hormones—this book doesn't offer tired solutions or rigid strategies. Instead, it offers presence, perspective and permission: permission to parent with empathy, to slow down and listen and to honour the transformation your daughter is undergoing.

Each chapter invites you into the hidden emotional landscapes behind the slammed doors, the sudden silence, the outbursts of rage and the moments of unexpected closeness. Through honest storytelling, poignant reflections and a compassionate lens, the author dismantles the myth that your daughter's struggles mean she's broken. She isn't spiralling out of control—she's navigating an internal maze of self-discovery and she's doing it the only way she knows how. When she shuts down, she may be overwhelmed. When she lashes out, she may be scared. When she pulls away, she may be craving space to figure out what feels right to her.

This is not a book of advice. It is a book of accompaniment. It is for the parent who lies awake wondering what happened to the bubbly little girl who once held their hand. It is for the mother who finds herself walking on eggshells. It is for the father who longs to connect but doesn't know where to begin. It is for anyone who has felt lost in the sea of mood swings, one-word answers and the ache of emotional distance. The guidance here is rooted in the belief that parenting a teenage girl isn't about fixing her—it's about learning to see her with new eyes. And in that seeing, there is the potential for deep healing, powerful reconnection and a trust that will carry your relationship forward, long after the storms have passed.

"She's Not Just Angry — She's Growing" is your reminder that your daughter's defiance may be a call for independence, her tears a longing for safety and her silence an invitation to sit beside her without demanding words. With gentle truths and empowering insight, this book helps you shift from control to connection, from discipline to dialogue and from reacting in fear to responding with love. Because she doesn't need you to have all the answers. She just needs you to stay—patient, open and unshaken—even when she pushes you away. And when you do, you'll both discover something extraordinary: that these turbulent years can be a bridge, not a battle. A journey, not a fight. And a chance to grow—**together**....

About the Author

The author of 'She's Not Just Angry — She's Growing' is, above all, a mother. Long before this book came to life, she was just a mom in the middle of it all, trying to understand and raise her daughter through the ups and downs of everyday life. She knows what it's like to lie awake at night worrying, to sit through long, silent car rides, to argue over small things that somehow feel huge and to feel the pain that lingers after a door is slammed shut. She's questioned herself more than once; did she say too much or maybe not enough?

But through all the struggles, she's also had the joy of watching her daughter grow—not just in age, but in strength, wisdom, and her true self.

She lives in a joint family, a mix of traditions and surprises, where the kitchen smells like dinner cooking, where voices overlap and love runs deep even when it's unspoken. She is the mother of two children and believes strongly in the beauty of joint family life. Her writing doesn't come from a place of perfection. It comes from real life; from sitting on the kitchen floor after a long day, from standing outside her daughter's locked door, from morning school drives and everyday chaos.

She doesn't claim to be an expert. She's simply a fellow mom, figuring things out one day at a time—just like the rest of us. Her stories are not perfectly told. They're real. They come from moments when tempers flared, feelings got hurt and healing had to happen. But they're also filled with hope; hope found in quiet apologies, laughter after tears and the strength that grows when a mother chooses love and understanding over being right.

She's learning, like we all are, that the best thing a mother can do is lead with gentleness, even when the world tells her to be tough.

This book is meant to be more than just something you read. She hopes it gives you a moment to pause, take a breath, and feel something soften in your heart. She hopes you'll remember that your daughter isn't pushing you away—she's trying to grow into the space she needs to become herself. And most of all, she hopes you'll feel a little less alone. Because none of us are doing this perfectly. But we are doing it—and we're doing it together…

Contents

The Eye Roll is Just the Beginning ----------------------------------9

Hormones, Headphones, Hysteria ---------------------------- 19

Not a Phase—A Transformation------------------------------ 29

Mood Swings and Mixed Signals ------------------------------ 36

From Meltdowns to Meaning------------------------------ 48

The Power of the Pause ------------------------------------ 59

Mirror: The Role of Self-Image ------------------------------ 71

Friends, Fights and Frenemies ------------------------------ 81

When She Pushes You Away ------------------------------ 92

Talking Without Triggering ------------------------------ 105

The Silent Tantrum------------------------------------ 117

Empathy Over Ego ------------------------------------ 129

Safe Spaces & Soft Landings------------------------------ 139

Rewriting the Story Together ------------------------------ 151

She's Becoming Her, Not You ------------------------------ 162

Acknowledgements ------------------------------------ 166

Chapter 1
The Eye Roll is Just the Beginning

I saw it before it even happened—the way her shoulders tensed, the quick sigh, the subtle narrowing of her eyes. And then, right on cue, came the eye roll. A full, sweeping, dramatic movement that only a teenage girl can perfect.

All I had done was ask my thirteen-year-old daughter, Kalpana, if she had packed her water bottle. A simple, everyday question. But to her, it must have felt like a personal attack.

"Yes, Maa," she replied, dragging the words as if I had wasted her precious time. She didn't wait for a response. She just turned and walked off into her room, leaving behind a stunned silence and a very confused mother holding a warm tiffin in the kitchen.

I stood there for a few seconds, blinking. Not angry. Just… puzzled. Where had my little girl gone? The one who used to come running to me after school, who'd climb into my lap to tell me about her day, who used to ask for two goodnight hugs *"just in case one didn't work."* That girl would never have walked away like this.

Over the next few days, I noticed more changes. Every small question became a trigger. When I reminded her about her homework, she snapped that I was micromanaging her. When I asked if she needed help braiding her hair, she said she wasn't five anymore. Even my concern— *"You've been quiet today"*—was met with frustration. *"You always say that. Can't I just be quiet?"*

I felt like I was walking on eggshells in my own home. Unsure what to say, when to say it or how not to be the enemy.

One evening, while folding clothes in the living room, I sat beside her as she watched a show. On screen, a teenage girl was yelling at her mother, *"You never listen! You only talk!"* Kalpana didn't react, but I could feel her shoulders stiffen. I asked gently, *"Do I do that too?"*

She hesitated, then shrugged. *"Sometimes. I mean... it's like... you assume things. Like you already know how I feel."*

That sentence stayed with me all night. She wasn't wrong. I did assume. I assumed she was being rude, not overwhelmed. I assumed she was angry, not exhausted. I assumed she was distant, not hurting. All this time, I was responding to her reactions, not reaching for her feelings.

The next morning, when Kalpana gave me her signature *"don't start"* look as she packed her bag, I didn't lecture her. I just said, *"I know mornings are hard. Thanks for getting everything ready on your own today."*

She didn't respond. But when I went to tidy her room later, I found a small sticky note on her desk. It simply said, *"Sorry I was snappy yesterday. I didn't sleep well. Thx for not making it a big deal."* Just a line. But for me, it was a door opening.

Now, when she sighs or rolls her eyes, I try not to take it personally. I try to remember that this is her trying to find herself. That she's not pushing me away to hurt me—she's pushing just to see if I'll still stay. If I'll still be here when the storm passes.

She is not just moody. She is not just dramatic. She is not just being **"difficult."** She is growing and testing her voice and trying to make space for who she's becoming.

The **eye roll**? It's not the end of the conversation. It's the start of a new kind of connection. A language where love shows up not through perfect moments, but through quiet patience. And I'm still learning to speak it.

The Shift No One Warns You About

No one truly warns you about this part of parenting—not the books, not the older parents, not even your own instincts. There's plenty of talk about toddler tantrums, the "**terrible twos**," and scraped knees. But no one tells you about the terrible tweens—the ones who no longer cry out loud but go silent. Whose emotions don't explode, but retreat. Whose eyes, once bright with constant questions and affection, now look past you with practiced indifference.

When our daughters are little, comfort feels simple. A hug fixes most things. A bedtime story, a cartoon, a lollipop—it all works. You can feel their hearts soften as you hold them. You know how to reach them.

But something shifts during adolescence. It's subtle at first. They start responding in one-word answers. They keep their doors closed more often. They roll their eyes at your jokes. Your touch no longer feels like home; it's something they flinch away from. And suddenly, you're unsure—about how to talk, how to help, even how to love them in a way they'll let you.

One evening, I was scrolling through my phone and came across a photo of Kalpana at eight—laughing in a princess dress, chocolate smeared across her face. That girl used to run into my arms when I returned from work. Now, I'm lucky if I get a half-hearted "**hmm**" from behind a phone screen.

And quietly, painfully, I began to wonder: Is this still a phase? Or am I losing her for good?

No one tells you about the self-doubt that follows. About how you'll question every decision you've made. About how you'll stare at her closed door, wondering if she's okay—and whether you're still her safe space.

But I've come to understand something: it's not rejection. It's growth. She's not pulling away because I failed her. She's pulling away because she's learning how to hold herself. It doesn't mean she doesn't need me. It just means she needs me differently.

It's Not Personal—Even If It Feels Like It Is

After a loud and exhausting argument over Kalpana's chaotic room, I found myself standing alone in the hallway, heart aching and ego bruised. Her room looked like a tornado had passed through it and my attempt to "**talk**" about it had quickly escalated into yelling. She had snapped, slammed the door and I was left questioning everything.

So, I called Pratibha, my friend and a gynaecologist, who also happens to be the mother of two daughters. *"She hates me,"* I said, tears in my eyes.

Pratibha laughed, kindly. *"No, she doesn't. She's 13. She's trying to figure herself out. And you, my friend, are her safest person. That's why she pushes—because she knows you'll still be there when the storm passes."* She added, *"This age is like Mumbai monsoon. Suddenly sunny, suddenly storm. Carry an umbrella and don't take it personally."*

That line floored me. What if it wasn't rejection… but trust in disguise?

Teenagers won't always cry or reach out when they're overwhelmed. Sometimes, they roll their eyes. Sometimes, they snap. Sometimes, they act like you're the problem—because you're the only one safe enough to fall apart with.

It doesn't make it easy. But it does mean that you're still home base—even when they act like you're the enemy. Their worst moods are often reserved for the person they trust most not to abandon them and that's you.

Later that night, Kalpana came to the kitchen, quiet and a little softer. She didn't say sorry. She just muttered, *"I cleaned up the desk."*

And I didn't ask for more. Because that was her way of saying: I still need you. I just didn't know how to say it without shouting earlier. And I was listening.

The Emotional Earthquake of Adolescence

Adolescence isn't just a phase—it's an emotional earthquake. Science confirms what mothers instinctively sense: that during these years, a girl's brain undergoes a massive neurological renovation. Think of it like a complete operating system upgrade—but the hardware is still fragile, the system keeps glitching and emotions are firing faster than reason can catch up.

The part of the brain responsible for logic, planning and impulse control—the prefrontal cortex—is still under construction. But the emotional centre, **the amygdala**? That's already on high alert. Which means your daughter is feeling everything deeply, intensely and often without filters—but she doesn't yet have the tools to fully explain why.

I experienced this firsthand on what should've been a harmless Tuesday.

Kalpana had gone out for the evening and I borrowed her shoes—the sparkly white ones she had just bought with her own pocket money. When she came home and saw me wearing them, she froze. Her lips tightened, her eyes widened and then came the sharp, unmistakable roll of the eyes, followed by a muttered, *"Seriously, Maa?"*

It wasn't about the shoes. It was about her sense of identity. Her growing desire for boundaries. Her unspoken need to feel in control of something—anything—in a world that suddenly felt confusing.

To me, it was just footwear. To her, it was something that belonged to her alone—a small piece of independence in a life where so much still feels monitored, managed and misunderstood.

And because she didn't have the words to say all of that, she responded with the only language available in that emotional moment: **the eye roll**. The tone. The silent treatment.

Teenage girls aren't trying to be dramatic. They're trying to survive the inner chaos that even they don't fully understand.

So now, when Kalpana snaps or retreats, I try to remember that this is not defiance. It's her brain and body struggling to catch up with each other. It's messy. It's loud. It's uncomfortable. But most of all—it's normal.

And if I can pause long enough to see the storm behind the sigh, I can respond not with hurt… but with grace. Because even earthquakes, with all their chaos, are signs of something shifting—something growing stronger underneath.

The Story Behind Her Silence

Some silences arrive dressed as indifference—but carry the weight of heartbreak. That's how it felt the evening Kalpana came home from school without saying a word. She walked in, dropped her bag with a soft thud and went straight to her room. No complaints, no sarcasm, not even the usual half-hearted *"I'm starving."*

I followed behind her with my typical string of gentle questions. *How was school today? Did you get the maths result? Everything okay?"*

All I got in return was a shrug, a barely audible *"fine,"* and eyes that didn't quite meet mine. The kind of answers that aren't meant to be rude, just... protective. Carefully designed to say nothing and everything at once.

Later that night, I found her curled up in bed, her hoodie pulled tightly over her head, facing the wall. Her birthday was a few days away. She had talked about it endlessly just last week—what cake she wanted, which friends she was inviting, even the colour of the balloons.

But now she lay there quiet, shoulders stiff, phone beside her—untouched.

I sat on the edge of the bed. I didn't ask again. I didn't touch her arm. I didn't offer tissue or tea. I just waited. After what felt like forever, her voice, cracked and low, slipped through the darkness: *"They made a separate group without me. Everyone was invited. They're having a sleepover on the same day."* There it was.

Not a tantrum. Not drama. Just a girl grieving something small but deeply personal belonging. That night, I learned something I'll carry forever: **Silence isn't always distance. Sometimes, it's fear wearing quiet like armour.**

Kalpana didn't need me to say, *"they're not worth it"* or *"you'll make new friends."* She didn't want a motivational speech or a problem-solving plan. She just needed one thing—my quiet, unconditional presence. So, I stayed. No pressure. No fixing. Just love.

Because behind every teenage silence is a story, waiting for the safety of stillness to come to the surface. And if we can learn to stop asking, stop rushing, stop needing them to "snap out of it"—we give them the one thing the world rarely offers: **Room to feel what they feel and still be fully held.**

Eye Rolls as Emotional Clues

One evening, I found Kalpana in tears over something that, at first glance, felt so small it almost made me laugh—I had folded her favourite t-shirt the *"wrong way."* Not ruined it, not stained it, not thrown it out. Just folded it. Poorly, according to her.

She walked into the room, saw the shirt on the bed and gasped. *"Why would you do that? You know I fold it inside out!"* I turned, confused. *"It's just a shirt."*

But then I saw her eyes fill—not with anger, but with that shaky kind of frustration that has very little to do with the thing in front of you. And that's when it hit me. This wasn't about cotton and creases.

It was everything else—school stress bubbling under the surface, unspoken friendship drama, the confusing storm of body changes, the pressure of expectations, the exhaustion of having to be "**fine**" all the time. The shirt was just the last thread holding her together that day.

I used to roll my eyes right back at hers. I used to take her sarcasm personally—her eye rolls, her clipped tone, her sudden withdrawal as signs of attitude. But slowly, I began to notice patterns.

The eye roll wasn't **rebellion**. It was a reflex. A shield. A silent cry. It often showed up when she felt embarrassed, overwhelmed or cornered. When something I said landed too close to a hidden insecurity. When she was unsure of herself but didn't want me to see it.

Her eye roll was her way of saying, *"I don't know how to handle this right now,"* without having to admit that she didn't have the words.

Now, when it happens, I take a breath instead of a stand. I pause instead of pounce. I ask myself quietly: Is she tired? Is she afraid I'm judging her? Did something at school throw her off? Is she just stretched too thin to handle correction right now?

It doesn't mean I let everything slide. But it does mean I try to listen more deeply—to the emotion beneath the reaction. It's not always easy. Some days I fail and snap back. But more and more, I'm learning to respond instead of reacting. Because that's where the real connection begins—not in fixing her behaviour, but in understanding the why behind it.

The eye roll, I now realise, isn't the end of a conversation. It's often the beginning of one—if I can stay soft enough to hear what she's not saying out loud.

The Beginning of a New Relationship

Kalpana is 15 now. And no—she hasn't outgrown the eye roll. She still sighs like the weight of the world rests on her shoulders. She still tells me I *"don't get it,"* that I'm *"so dramatic,"* that I *"overthink everything."* But something's shifted. Something small, invisible, but deeply real.

Now, when I knock on her door and ask if she wants to talk, she sometimes says **yes**. Not always. But sometimes. And those **"sometimes"** feel like miracles.

She opens up—not all at once, not in perfect language—but she shares. She tells me about the things that make her anxious before exams. About friends she's not sure are friends anymore. About a boy who makes her nervous and happy at the same time. About feeling too much, too often and not knowing what to do with it all. And when I ask her, gently, what changed—what helped her start talking again—she said something so simple and honest it caught my breath.

"You stopped trying to fix me. You just started sitting with me."

That sentence undid something inside me. Because for so long, I thought my job was to hold her together. To offer advice. To **"solve"** every emotional mess. But all she really needed was someone who didn't flinch when she was messy. Someone who didn't try to edit her feelings. Someone who could sit beside her—not above her—with quiet understanding.

And that's when I realised: **The eye roll was never the enemy. It was the beginning.** The beginning of her figuring out who she was. The beginning of me learning how to mother a girl becoming a woman. The beginning of us building a new kind of closeness—not rooted in constant conversation, but in quiet permission. Permission to feel. Permission to fail. Permission to come undone… and still be loved completely.

This is what no one tells you—there's a new relationship waiting on the other side of the eye rolls and slammed doors. It's softer. Wiser.

Built on mutual respect instead of control. Not the mother-child bond of before, but something braver—the bond of two humans learning how to meet in the middle. And that? That is more than I ever hoped for.

Chapter 2

Hormones, Headphones, Hysteria

The first time Kalpana cried in the bathroom for no clear reason, she came out not looking sad—but angry. Her face was red, her eyes puffy and she looked like she wanted to throw something across the room. But when I asked gently, *"Are you okay, beta?"* she snapped, *"I don't even know why I'm crying! Just leave me alone!"* Then she slammed the door of her room, left her dinner untouched and disappeared into her headphones for the rest of the evening.

That was the first time I really felt like I didn't know how to help my own daughter.

Kalpana used to be someone who narrated her whole day to me—who ate biscuits while sitting on the kitchen counter, who once cried because a butterfly flew away too fast. Now all I got were grunts, deep sighs and long hours of silence. It wasn't just the mood swings—it was the confusion behind them. One moment, she was dancing in the living room, laughing at a reel. The next, she was curled up on her bed, face buried in a pillow, telling me to stop asking so many questions.

I began to realise this wasn't personal. It was biological. Her body was changing. Her brain was rewiring itself. Hormones were rising and falling like a roller coaster and Kalpana herself didn't know where the seatbelt was.

One evening, after yet another door-slam moment, I sat down beside her outside the balcony, not to lecture her, but just to be nearby. After a few quiet minutes, she finally whispered, *"It's like my head is full all the time. Like I'm feeling too much and nothing at the same time."*

That sentence stayed with me. Because how do you help a child who can't even explain what she's feeling? How do you comfort someone who's building walls and doesn't know how to open the gate again?

I had to unlearn a lot of what I thought motherhood meant during those days. I stopped giving constant advice. I stopped reacting instantly to every sigh or sharp word. I started waiting. Sitting beside her, not saying much, just letting her know I was still there. I began texting her things I used to say aloud. *"I'm here if you want to talk. I love you, even when you're quiet. Want to go for a walk later?"*

There were days she replied with nothing but a thumbs-up emoji. But even that felt like a small victory. Slowly, I also began noticing the patterns. She wasn't rude—she was overwhelmed. She wasn't lazy—she was tired. She wasn't uninterested—she was distracted by a hundred thoughts she couldn't name. Her headphones became her protection, her hoodie became her shield and her diary became her therapist.

At night, when she thought I couldn't hear, she played the same song on repeat, as if the lyrics were holding her emotions for her. And in the mornings, she walked around the house like her body was too heavy for her soul. I stopped pushing her to talk. I started giving her space and kindness. I reminded myself that growing up isn't always graceful—it's messy, noisy, confusing.

One night, I peeked into her room while she was asleep. Her face looked so soft, so peaceful, like the little girl she once was. I sat at the edge of her bed, ran my fingers through her hair and whispered, *"You're not lost, Kalpana. You're just changing. And I'm still here."*

She didn't hear me. But I think she felt it. Because the next morning, she came to the kitchen, took her tea and said softly, *"Sorry for shouting yesterday. I wasn't okay."* Then she went back to her room, headphones on. But for the first time in weeks, she left the door slightly open.

And I knew: she's still in there. Still my daughter. Just finding her way through the storm of hormones and headphones. And I would be her calm—until she finds her own.

Inside the Teenage Brain

If parenting a teenage girl feels like navigating a storm without a map, there's a reason: her brain is being completely rewired behind the scenes.

When puberty begins, it's not just her body that changes—her brain starts a full renovation. But unlike renovations that come with contractors and blueprints, this one arrives with no instructions, no predictable timeline and no off-switch.

The emotional regions of her brain—especially the **amygdala**—suddenly become hyperactive. This is the area that processes fear, joy, shame, jealousy and all those big, confusing emotions. It lights up like a festival during adolescence, making everything feel louder, brighter and heavier.

But the part of her brain that helps her slow down, think clearly, plan ahead—the **prefrontal cortex**—is still slowly under construction. That means while she feels everything in vivid, overwhelming detail, her ability to pause, reflect and regulate hasn't fully caught up.

So, when she snaps over something small or bursts into tears mid-conversation or acts like the world is ending because of a slight text from a friend—it's not overreaction for the sake of drama. It's her brain trying to make sense of feelings it doesn't yet know how to hold.

Understanding this changes how we respond. Instead of saying, *"You're being too sensitive,"* we can say, *"That felt big, didn't it?"* Instead of trying to fix her reaction, we can offer her tools to name what she's feeling. Because helping her recognise an emotion is the first step toward managing it.

And no—she won't always get it right. She'll misread situations. She'll overthink. She'll freeze or flare up when her brain feels flooded. But that doesn't mean she's broken.

It means she's becoming. And what she needs most is a steady adult nearby—someone who doesn't meet her chaos with more chaos but with calm curiosity.

Because one day that slowly forming prefrontal cortex will catch up. Her emotions will stop running ahead of her voice. She'll look back and thank you—not for making her perfect, but for staying steady while she learned how to be whole.

The Hormone Rollercoaster

I called Pratibha that evening in sheer exhaustion. *"She's always moody, yaar. For one second, she's fine, the next she's crying or yelling. I ask her to eat, she snaps. I ask if she's okay, she rolls her eyes. It's like I don't even know her anymore."*

Pratibha, ever the calm and seasoned voice of reason laughed gently. *"Welcome to puberty dear. Her hormones are like traffic in Delhi—chaotic, unpredictable and completely out of control."*

She explained how Kalpana's brain and body were changing at a speed she couldn't keep up with. Estrogen, progesterone and a whole cocktail of other hormones were surging through her system, tugging at her mood, energy, sleep and sense of control—all at once.

"She's not doing this to irritate you," Pratibha said. *"She's confused too. Her body feels unfamiliar. Her mind's running ahead of her words. She doesn't even understand half of what she's feeling."*

That hit me hard. Because in that moment, I saw Kalpana not as defiant—but as overwhelmed. She wasn't trying to be difficult and to stay afloat in a body and brain that felt new every single day. And suddenly, I wasn't angry anymore. I was… protective. Curious. A little heartbroken, too.

Because the mood swings, the tears, the sharp tone—it wasn't about me. It was about her navigating an emotional rollercoaster without a seatbelt.

These hormonal shifts can cause:

- *Sudden mood changes that even she doesn't understand*
- *Disturbed sleep or sleeping too much*
- *Sensitivity to things that didn't bother her before*
- *Anxiety, self-doubt or unexpected fear*
- *Physical discomfort like cramps, fatigue or constant headaches*

And though the science makes it sound clinical, living with it feels anything but. But once I understood the "*why,*" my response began to shift. Instead of reacting with "*Why are you like this?*" I started asking, "*Want some water?*" or "*Do you want to be alone for a bit?*"

Not always. Not perfectly. But more and more, I started meeting the chaos with calm. Because she didn't need correction in that moment. She needed understanding—and a mother who remembered that inside all that fire and frustration was still the little girl learning how to grow into her own skin.

Headphones - A Temporary Escape

The headphones became a wall between us. Not literal noise-cancelling ones, but the invisible kind that teenage girls wear like Armor—soft on the outside but built to keep the world at a safe distance.

It was a lazy Sunday. The kind where we used to cook together, laugh about nothing or fight over who got the last piece of toast. I missed those days. I thought maybe I could bring a little of that back. So, I walked to her room and knocked gently.

"What would you like for lunch?" I asked. She didn't look up from her phone. *"Anything,"* she said flatly, one earbud still in. *"No mood for Aloo Parantha?"* I tried again, a little more playful. She shrugged. *"Whatever."*

And that was it. No smile. No eye contact. No warmth. Just the sound of typing and the low hum of music that clearly didn't include me. I stood there for a second longer than I should have, trying not to look wounded. I wanted to say, *"Beta, please talk to me. Just a few words. I miss you. Why are you like this now?"* But I didn't.

Instead, I quietly turned and walked back to the kitchen, pretending everything was fine. I chopped onions while blinking back tears. Because what no one prepares you for is how rejection doesn't always come with raised voices or slammed doors. Sometimes it comes in the form of distance—a quiet **"whatever,"** a distracted nod or the slow fade of a child who once told you everything… now telling you nothing.

And you wonder—when did I stop being her favourite person? When did **"Maa"** become background noise? But that day, as I wiped my eyes and placed the dough back in the bowl, something shifted inside me. I reminded myself—this isn't the end. It's a pause. A moment in time. A messy, painful, necessary growing space.

Those headphones? They weren't shutting me out. They were letting her tune out the world that often feels too loud, too demanding, too complicated to explain. And even if I'm not the soundtrack she wants to hear right now—I'll be here, waiting in the kitchen, always ready to listen when she decides to take them off. Because one day, she will and when she does, I'll be right here—making aloo parathas. Just like before.

When the Hysteria Hits

It was a regular Wednesday. I was tidying up Kalpana's study table—just dusting, arranging a few books, trying to clear the wrappers and chaos that had accumulated. In the middle of it all, I found a small notebook, slightly worn on the edges. Thinking it was a rough pad;I flipped it open to check if it could be reused for grocery lists.

Within seconds, I realised it wasn't just paper. It was her diary. I closed it right away. I hadn't read more than a line. But the guilt hit instantly. That evening, when she came home and noticed it had been moved, her face changed. *"You touched my diary?"* she asked sharply.

I opened my mouth to explain—but before I could speak, the explosion came. *"That's private! You don't respect anything that's mine! Why would you even open it?!"*

Tears welled up. Her voice cracked. Her whole body trembled—not with rage, but with something closer to hurt and helplessness. I tried to calm her down, stumbling through explanations. *"I didn't read it, beta. I just opened it by mistake. I thought it was an old notebook. I swear."*

But she wasn't hearing any of it. *"You don't get it!"* she shouted. *"This is why I don't tell you anything!"* And just like that, she walked off, slamming the door behind her. To me, it was a misunderstanding. To her, it was a violation.

Her diary wasn't just paper and ink. It was her only safe space to feel without being seen. And in her world—full of shifting friendships, changing moods and constant self-doubt—privacy feels like power. Control. Safety.

I sat with the weight of it that evening. I didn't chase her. I didn't text her. I waited. Later that night, after dinner, I knocked on her door. She didn't say "come in," but she didn't stop me either. I sat beside her on the bed and said quietly, *"I wasn't trying to invade your space. I should've been more careful. I'm really sorry."*

She didn't speak at first. But then she said, in a voice so soft I almost missed it: *"It's not just the diary. I feel like I'm losing control of everything lately. And when something like this happens, it just… breaks me."*

That's when I understood—the hysteria isn't about the thing. It's about the wave that's been building quietly behind her eyes all week long. The outburst is just the point where everything spills. What she needs most in that moment isn't fixing. It's someone to hold space for the flood.

And that night, by saying less and listening more, I gave her exactly that. A place to fall apart… without fear. And slowly, I saw her putting the pieces back—this time, not alone.

How I Learned to Ride the Waves

There was a time I used to panic every time Kalpana had an outburst. Her spirals—those intense waves of frustration, sadness or complete shutdown—used to catch me off guard. I'd either rush to fix it or get pulled in emotionally and react. But over time, I've learned something essential: I can't stop the waves… but I can learn to ride them.

Here's what I try to do now when the storm starts to swell:

Stay calm – because if I lose it too, the fire gets bigger. She's already overwhelmed. If I meet her heat with mine, it only adds fuel. So now, when she shouts or slams doors, I take a deep breath and remind myself: This isn't about me. My calm doesn't solve everything, but it creates a steady presence she can come back to when the flood settles.

Say less – because sometimes, silence is the safest thing. Teenagers don't always need advice. In the middle of the emotional chaos, my explanations, logic or *"what you should do"* speeches only make her feel more misunderstood. So instead, I sit beside her—quietly. I let the air settle. Being present without pushing words is often the loudest kind of love.

Remind her she's not broken. She already feels confused, out of control, maybe even ashamed for *"overreacting."* So, I try to anchor her in compassion. I say things like, *"It's okay to feel this. I'm here. You don't have to explain."* These words are small, but they say: You are not too much. You are not failing.

Offer comfort – not correction. I bring her a warm cup of milk, a snack she likes or just hand her a blanket. No questions. No judgment. Just care. Because sometimes, it's not deep conversation that brings her back—it's the quiet, physical comfort that tells her, you are still safe. Still loved.

Check in later – after the storm passes. Once the air is clear and her body has calmed down, we talk. Not right away and not always deeply—but I gently ask, *"Want to tell me what was really going on?"* And when she's ready, she shares. Sometimes a lot. Sometimes just a line. But every word is a little thread that keeps us connected.

I still get it wrong. I still lose patience. But slowly, I'm learning to stop being afraid of the waves. I'm learning that my steadiness matters more than my solutions. Because she doesn't need a lifeguard shouting from the shore. She needs a quiet boat beside her, riding every wave until she finds the shore again. And I can be that. I am that.

What's Beautiful in the Mess

This stage of life? It's loud. It's unpredictable. It's full of slammed doors, stretched silences, eye rolls and emotions that swing from joy to heartbreak in the span of a single hour. It's messy. It's maddening.

But it's also quietly, profoundly beautiful. Because what I've come to realise is that this isn't just a phase to survive—it's a sacred chapter of becoming. Not just for Kalpana, but for me too. Every meltdown, every headphone retreat, every unexpected hug or whispered apology—it all means something. None of it is wasted. She's not broken. She's blooming, even when it looks like falling apart.

She's not just growing taller—she's growing inward. Stretching into the uncomfortable shape of who she's meant to be. It takes time. It takes space. And it takes an unreasonable amount of grace, for both of us.

This chapter of parenting isn't about control. It isn't about rules or consequences or "fixing her attitude." It's about learning to pause instead of react. It's about choosing presence over power. It's about remembering that even on her worst days—especially on her worst days—she's still figuring out how to carry the weight of who she's becoming.

Her anger? It's not always about me. Her silence? It's not rejection—it's reflection. Her music? Not noise. Not rebellion. It's her comfort. Her language. Her anchor. And those tears? The ones she tries to hide or releases in sudden floods. They are not weakness. They are bravery. Proof that she still feels deeply, still hopes, still trusts me enough to unravel in front of me.

So yes, this stage is wild. But hidden in the storm is something stunning: A girl finding her voice. A mother learning to listen. A bond growing not through perfection—but through presence.

She's growing and so am I. And even in the mess… there's so much beauty to hold on to.

Chapter 3

Not a Phase — A Transformation

There was a time when Kalpana used to copy everything I did. She'd wear my dupatta, pretend to talk on the phone the way I did, even try applying lotion on her face the exact same way. If I wore green, she wanted green. If I cooked upma, she wanted to **"help"** by stirring, even if it made more mess than progress.

But these days, she doesn't want to be anything like me. She chooses clothes that I don't understand, music I can't relate to and opinions that sometimes feel like little challenges—testing whether I'll accept the person she's becoming or just keep trying to pull her back to the version I liked better.

One afternoon, while we were going through old photos for a family collage, Kalpana picked up a picture of herself when she was about seven—hair in two neat ponytails, smiling shyly in a frilly frock. She looked at it and said, *"I feel bad for that girl. She had no idea what she'd grow into."*

I laughed softly and asked, *"What do you mean?"* She shrugged. *"I don't know… I'm just… different now. I don't know who I am half the time."* It hit me then—this wasn't a phase.

This was a shift. A full-blown, deep, invisible transformation happening inside her. Not just hormones or moods—but identity. Kalpana was no longer the child who wanted to fit into everything. She was now a teenager trying to break out of everything—every label, every expectation, even parts of herself that no longer fit.

I used to think these changes were temporary. That the eye rolls, the need for privacy, the strong opinions, the sudden silences—they were all just passing clouds. But they're not clouds. They're signs of a whole new season.

There's a certain sadness to it, as a mother. Watching her outgrow bedtime cuddles. Seeing her replace fairy tales with feminist poetry. Listening to her talk about the world with both wonder and weariness in her voice. Sometimes I look at her and think—I miss the little girl. But then I remind myself—this girl, this version, is still mine too. Just… **evolving**.

The hardest part of parenting a teenager isn't the rebellion or the mood swings. It's the letting go. Letting go of the child you once knew, so you can meet the young woman she's becoming. And that takes courage. Not just for her. But for me too.

One day, I asked her, *"Do you ever feel confused about who you are?"* She was lying on the sofa, scrolling through her phone, but she paused and nodded. *"All the time,"* she said. *"I feel like I'm stuck between too many versions of myself. The one you see, the one my friends know and the one I only show to me."*

That's when I realised—Kalpana wasn't pretending. She wasn't being dramatic. She was simply becoming. Day by day. Quietly. Boldly. Clumsily. It's easy to dismiss teenage behaviour as **"just a phase."** But if we keep calling it that, we miss the chance to witness the transformation.

We miss the moments where they start standing up for themselves. Where they question things, we never dared to. Where they make mistakes, feel deeply and then try again. Kalpana is not the same girl she was last year and she won't be the same girl next year either.

And that's not something to fear. It's something to honour. So, these days, when she rolls her eyes or shuts her door, I remind myself—it's not rejection. It's redefinition. It's her way of saying, *"I need space to grow into myself."* And my job is to give her that space… while staying just close enough so she knows she's never growing alone.

The "Who Am I?" Years

When Kalpana was little, she wore our love like a label. *"I'm Mumma's girl,"* she would say proudly. She copied my mannerisms, laughed at her father's jokes like I did and followed our rules without question. But somewhere around thirteen, something subtle but powerful began to shift.

She started to question. Everything.

She pushed back when I reminded her to clean her room. She rolled her eyes when I called her "*beta*" in public. She started using phrases like, *"Stop treating me like a baby,"* or *"Just because you think it's right doesn't mean I do."* Her tone changed. Her clothing choices changed. Her sense of certainty faded and a new self-awareness took its place.

At first, I took it personally. I wondered if I had done something wrong—if she was rejecting me or distancing herself out of anger. But slowly, I came to realise something far more meaningful: she wasn't trying to push me away. She was trying to pull herself forward.

Adolescence is not just physical; it's deeply emotional and psychological. Kalpana wasn't just growing taller—she was outgrowing the safety of simple definitions. She was searching for who she was beyond being someone's daughter, beyond the neat titles of "**student**," "**nice girl**," or "**responsible child**."

This self-searching is a messy, emotional and sometimes painful process. It can feel lonely for both of us. But it's also deeply necessary. It's how she learns to think for herself. It's how she builds an identity that isn't borrowed but earned.

Now, when she says, *"I don't know who I am,"* I try not to jump in with answers. I sit beside her and let her feel the confusion. Because in those moments of not knowing, she's not lost—she's growing.

The "New Version" of Her

It happened quietly one afternoon. I found Kalpana crying while scrolling through Instagram reels, her face lit by the pale glow of the screen.

"What happened, beta?" I asked gently, sitting next to her. She wiped her eyes and said, *"Everyone's so pretty and confident. I feel like I don't even know what I like anymore."*

In that moment, she looked like a contradiction—both fragile and strong, young and wise, child and almost-woman. I wanted to rush in with affirmations. Of course you're beautiful! I wanted to say. Don't compare yourself to them! But I didn't.

Instead, I took a breath, hugged her and said, *"You're figuring it out. It's okay not to have all the answers."* Because the truth is, this age isn't about being sure. It's about the very opposite.

Kalpana is trying things on—not just clothes or makeup, but ideas, moods, even personalities. She's experimenting. Failing. Getting back up. She's discovering what she loves and what she doesn't. And some days, that process feels overwhelming.

She will outgrow some versions of herself. She might say she loves singing one month and avoid it the next. That's not inconsistency—it's exploration. And our job as parents is to hold space for that exploration without judgement or panic.

So now, when I see her shift, I remind myself—she's not being dramatic. She's discovering who she is. And that is sacred work.

The Closet Makeover

Last Diwali, Kalpana came to me with a request that caught me off guard. *"Mumma, can I wear a plain T-shirt this year instead of a lehenga?"* I looked up, surprised. *"You love dressing up for Diwali!"* She shrugged. *"I don't feel like looking girly anymore."*

My first instinct was to label it a phase. But then I paused. I remembered the year I refused to wear Salwars and insisted on jeans. I remembered the time I cut my long hair short just because I wanted to feel different. She wasn't rebelling. She was reimagining herself.

That T-shirt was more than fabric. It was her way of saying, *"Let me decide how I want to show up in the world."* And in that moment, I had a choice. I could push back or I could honour her voice. So, I smiled and said, *"That T-shirt will look great on my princess."*

Her shoulders relaxed. She nodded, quietly pleased. And maybe, for a second, she felt seen. Not just as my daughter but as her own person.

We often think identity is built in big moments. But sometimes, it's born in the small choices—what to wear, how to speak, what music to love. And when we support those choices, we give them permission to keep exploring who they are becoming.

When They Pull Away

There was a time Kalpana used to narrate her entire day to me. From whom she sat with at lunch to how many likes she got on her latest post, she would bubble with stories. Now? I get half-sentences. Shrugs. Sometimes, just silence. One evening, I finally asked, *"Why don't you talk to me like you used to?"*

She didn't hesitate. *"Because you always give advice. Sometimes I just want you to listen."* Her words stung. But they were honest. In that moment, I realised that she didn't stop trusting me. She was just learning to trust herself.

Teenage girls don't always want answers. They want space to think their own thoughts, feel their own feelings and solve their own problems. What feels like distance isn't rejection. It's independence unfolding. And if we can sit in that space without demanding closeness, they eventually find their way back—on their own terms.

Now, when Kalpana pulls away, I don't chase. I stay nearby. Open. Unoffended. Because that's what she needs most: a mother who doesn't vanish when she withdraws. And when she does return—with a meme, a question or just to sit in the same room—I know she still trusts me.

From Obedient to Opinionated

It happened during dinner. Kalpana's grandfather was sharing his views on how girls should always dress modestly. She put her fork down, looked him straight in the eye and said, *"Dadu, I don't agree with that."* The room went quiet. Everyone looked at me.

My first instinct was to jump in. To tell her to respect elders, to not speak out so bluntly. But I paused. Because she wasn't yelling. She wasn't rude. She was thinking for herself. And isn't that the kind of daughter I want?

A girl who speaks her mind, even when it's uncomfortable. A girl who doesn't shrink to fit expectations. A girl who knows she has a right to her own beliefs. So instead of correcting her, I said, *"Okay. Tell me what you think instead."* Her face lit up. Not because I agreed, but because I gave her the one thing every young woman needs: **a voice that's heard without interruption.**

That night, I saw a glimpse of the woman she's becoming. And I felt proud. Not because she was obedient, but because she was brave.

A Beautiful, Messy Becoming

Teenagerhood is often misunderstood. We talk about it like a crisis, like something to "**get through**."

But it's not a disease. It's a doorway. It's the moment a girl begins to leave behind childhood and slowly steps into her own skin. It's clumsy. It's emotional. It's beautifully unpredictable.

One day, Kalpana is gossiping about friends. The next, she's drawing galaxies and writing poems in the corners of notebooks. One moment she wants me to sit beside her. The next, she shrugs me off like I'm the most embarrassing person in the world.

And honestly? It's confusing. For her and for me also.

But what I've come to understand is that all this inconsistency is not chaos. It's transformation. Like a caterpillar in a cocoon, she's slowly becoming something new.

And my job? Not to rush it. Not to define it. But to witness it with love.

I'm learning to loosen my grip. To stop pulling on her wings. To trust that she will emerge in her own time. Because she is becoming. And so am I. And that is its own quiet kind of miracle.

Chapter 4

Mood Swings and Mixed Signals

Some days, Kalpana wakes up humming a song, making herself tea and chatting about her favourite playlist. And some days—like yesterday—she walks around like a thundercloud, snapping at the spoon drawer for making too much noise.

I never know which version of her I'm going to meet. It used to worry me. A lot. I'd go over my words from the day before, wondering if *I had said something wrong. Did I forget to remind her of something? Was she upset with me or with herself?*

But more and more, I've realised this isn't about one moment, one mistake or one person.

It's about emotions she doesn't yet have the words for. Teenage girls feel everything with such intensity—**joy, irritation, jealousy, anxiety.** But they're still learning how to label those feelings, how to talk about them without sounding "dramatic", how to not feel embarrassed about feeling too much.

One afternoon, after a particularly sharp exchange about her screen time, Kalpana suddenly blurted out, *"I don't know why I'm like this! I get angry and I don't even want to. I hate it. I hate myself for it."*

That stopped me in my tracks. She wasn't being rude. She was overwhelmed. And beneath all that attitude was something very raw—confusion. Guilt. Fear.

So, I said softly, *"It's okay to not know what you're feeling sometimes. You're allowed to have messy days."* Her face softened, just a little. She didn't respond right away, but I knew she heard me.

I started changing the way I spoke to her after that. Instead of asking, *"Why are you in a mood today?"*, I'd ask,

"Is it one of those days where you just need space?"

Instead of saying, *"You're overreacting,"* I'd say,

"This seems like a lot right now. Want to take a break?"

Slowly, I watched Kalpana become less defensive and more honest.

One evening, she came to me and said, *"I'm not mad, I'm just… overwhelmed. School, friends, everything—it's just too much sometimes."*

That one sentence felt like a win. Because teenage girls don't need you to fix their moods. They need you to give those moods room to breathe.

It's easy to label them as moody or emotional. But the truth is, they're just emotionally full—and they don't know where to put it all. Some of it spills out as sarcasm. Some as silence. Some as unexpected tears.

I've learned to not always ask *"What's wrong?"*

Instead, I sit with her quietly. Or I leave her a snack with a note. Or I send her a message that just says, *"You don't have to talk. Just letting you know I'm here."*

And over time, she's started doing the same.

One evening after a long office day, I came home feeling completely drained. Kalpana noticed. She didn't ask anything. She just made tea and placed it next to me on the table with a soft *"I didn't put sugar—thought you'd want to add it yourself."*

That was her way of saying: *I see you too.*

These days, when her mood shifts without warning, I don't panic. I wait. I give her the gift of not needing to explain everything perfectly.

And in doing so, I'm teaching her something far more important than how to "behave."

I'm teaching her how to feel. How to name what she feels. How to honour it and eventually, how to move through it—without shame. Because emotional storms aren't something to silence. They're something to understand.

And if she learns to face her feelings now, gently, without fear… She'll grow into a woman who knows how to carry them with strength and softness both.

The Time She Cried Over Ice Cream

One day, I brought home her favourite—Naturals Tender Coconut Ice Cream. I'd picked it up thinking it would cheer her up, a small, sweet surprise in the middle of an ordinary day. I placed it on the table with a smile and called out, *"Look what I got for you!"*

Kalpana looked at it, blinked and suddenly her face crumpled. She started crying. Not loud sobs. Just quiet tears that caught me completely off guard. I stood there, ice cream tub in hand, confused and helpless. *"Beta, what happened?"*

She looked at me, barely above a whisper and said, *"Aap ye sab tabhi leke aate ho jab mujhe khani nahi hoti."* Then she turned and walked into her room, leaving me standing in a pool of silence.

I didn't know what to make of it. Guilt, confusion, hurt—all of it swirled inside me. It was just ice cream, wasn't it? Later that night, I found her curled up on her bed. I didn't ask anything, just sat beside her. After a while, she whispered, *"I had a bad day and the ice cream made me feel like I didn't deserve anything nice."*

That broke me. Because I realised in that moment—it was never about the ice cream. It was about how emotions sneak up when they're already piled high. How, in adolescence, even a kind gesture can feel unbearable when the heart is heavy.

Kalpana wasn't being dramatic. She wasn't ungrateful. She was overwhelmed. She just didn't have the words to explain it. And that's when I understood—sometimes, the most **fragile** moments come dressed as overreactions. And our job isn't to correct them. It's to hold them gently, with patience and love.

Giving Her the Vocabulary

I used to meet Kalpana's mood swings with questions like, *"What's wrong with you?"* or *"Why are you acting like this?"* I thought I was opening the door to conversation. But all I really did was push her further into silence. My tone wasn't curious—it was loaded. And in her world, where everything already felt big and messy, those questions felt more like pressure than comfort.

One day, after a particularly tense evening, I tried something different. I walked into her room, sat at the edge of her bed and instead of asking what was wrong, I gently asked, *"What are you feeling right now? Is it sadness? Anger? Are you frustrated? Or just… confused?"*

She rolled her eyes—of course she did. *"Mujhe nahi pta,"* she muttered, turning away. But that small shift in language planted something. It told her I wasn't there to interrogate—I was there to understand.

Over the next few weeks, I kept using those words. Not forcefully. Just offering them as options, like a menu of emotions she was allowed to pick from.

And slowly, she started answering.

"I feel irritated… but I don't know why."

"I'm tired. Not sleepy tired—just tired of being judged."

"I'm sad, but I don't want to talk about it. Not now."

Each time, I didn't rush to fix anything. I just nodded. Sometimes I said, *"Thank you for telling me."* Sometimes I simply sat beside her and said nothing. And that's when it clicked: When she named the emotion, she gained power over it.

It wasn't just a cloud above her head anymore. It had a name. A shape. A sound. It was no longer this mysterious storm swirling inside her—it was something she could sit with. Even if she didn't want to "**solve**" it right away, just knowing what it was made it less scary.

I've learned that emotional vocabulary isn't something girls magically develop at thirteen. It has to be taught, offered and modelled. So now, I name my own emotions in front of her too.

"I felt overwhelmed at work today."

"I'm disappointed with how a conversation went."

"I'm feeling a little fragile right now."

The more I said it, the safer she felt to say it too. And slowly, our house became a space where feelings weren't judged or dismissed. They were just... **heard**.

Because sometimes, the most important parenting tool isn't advice or discipline. It's a simple set of words. The kind that helps a teenage girl realise she's not broken—she's just learning how to speak her heart.

When She Pushed Everyone Away

It started with small things—snapping at her younger brother, rolling her eyes at Dadi, walking away when I asked if she wanted chai. But by the second week of Kalpana's exams, everything felt like it was triggering her. Every voice. Every noise. Every kind gesture somehow landed wrong.

She was angry at everything—and everyone.

One afternoon, after she shouted at me for asking if she had eaten lunch, I lost my patience. *"Why are you always angry these days?"* I asked, my tone sharper than it should've been.

She turned around, face flushed with frustration and shouted, *"Because I have too much in my head and I can't switch it off!"*

Her voice cracked a little at the end. And suddenly, the heat of the moment melted into something else—fear, exhaustion, pressure—all tangled up in that one sentence.

That was the moment I realised: her anger wasn't about us. It wasn't personal.

It was the language of overwhelm.

In that moment, I had two choices. I could match her frustration. Or I could meet her where she was—tired, tangled and silently begging for space.

So, I took a breath and said quietly, *"Okay. Want to take a walk?"*

She didn't answer. She didn't even look at me. I took that as a no and walked away, choosing to leave the door open instead of slamming it shut with my own emotions.

Later that evening, as I folded clothes in the living room, she quietly walked in and sat beside me. No words. No explanation. Just her presence, close enough to mean: I'm not okay, but I don't want to be alone.

I didn't say anything either. I just handed her a towel to fold. She took it without a word. And that silent exchange, that moment of shared stillness—that was enough.

I've learned that when a teenager pushes everyone away, what she's often saying is: *"I don't know how to handle what I'm feeling. I don't have space for anyone else's expectations right now."*

And the kindest thing we can do is not react with hurt—but with patience. To understand that pushing people away is sometimes their way of protecting the little energy they have left.

That night, Kalpana didn't need advice. She didn't need a motivational speech or reminders about gratitude.

She just needed a moment of quiet connection. No pressure. No judgement. No fixing.

Just someone willing to stay close, even when she couldn't explain why she felt so far away.

Learning to Not Fix Everything

For a long time, I believed that being a good mother meant offering answers. That my role, especially during Kalpana's teenage years, was to ease her stress, remove her pain and help her navigate through every emotional challenge with direction. So, I became a problem-solver—quick to give advice, quicker to reassure and always ready to speak when emotions were high.

If she came home upset from school, I'd encourage her to talk it out with her friend. If she was worried about marks, I'd remind her of her strengths. If she seemed overwhelmed, I'd try to put things into perspective, to calm her down. It was always about helping her **"get over it."**

But I started noticing something: she wasn't feeling better. In fact, she was getting quieter. Colder. More distant.

And then, one day, she burst out in frustration—not just at the situation, but at me. And while her words were sharp, what stayed with me was the emotion behind them: the exhaustion of constantly being told to fix her feelings before she was even ready to understand them.

That moment became a mirror. I realised I was doing what I thought was nurturing, but I was invalidating her experience. I was so focused on removing her discomfort that I never gave her permission to simply feel it.

So, I started stepping back. It wasn't easy. Every part of me wanted to help. But instead of jumping in with reassurance or logic, I began offering something simpler: presence. Quiet, steady, non-demanding presence.

I taught myself to listen without interrupting. To sit without filling the silence. To allow her tears without rushing to dry them. To offer comfort without conditions.

It felt strange at first. Passive, almost. But slowly, I began to see something remarkable: she started letting me in. Not for solutions, but for safety. Not to be guided out of the dark, but to know someone was willing to sit in it with her.

That shift changed everything. It taught me that emotional support isn't always about guidance—it's about creating space. Space where she can figure things out on her own. Where she learns that her feelings, no matter how messy or unclear, are allowed to exist without judgment or immediate resolution.

Now, when she closes her door or slumps onto the couch after a hard day, I don't rush in with answers. I keep the room warm, the air soft. I let her know I'm nearby. I might bring her tea, a blanket or just quietly begin folding clothes beside her.

Sometimes we don't even speak. And yet, those silent moments carry more weight than a dozen well-meant pieces of advice.

Because now I understand that she doesn't need me to fix her emotions. She needs to feel strong enough to sit with them and she needs someone who believes she can. That's what I offer her now—not solutions, but space. Not noise, but presence. Not a way out, but a place to be.

When Happy and Sad Coexist

It was just another evening, nothing special—just the two of us watching a light-hearted movie, a bowl of popcorn between us, her feet curled under a blanket. We were laughing together, for a moment in sync, like the old days before everything became so… layered.

But somewhere halfway through the film, I noticed her expression change. The laughter faded and tears began quietly streaming down her cheeks. No dramatic sobs. Just silent, sudden tears.

I glanced at her, unsure. It wasn't a sad scene. In fact, it was a silly one. She noticed me looking and quickly wiped her face. A soft chuckle escaped her lips, like she was trying to laugh at herself. But it wasn't humorous. It was bewildered, almost apologetic.

That moment stayed with me. Because it revealed something essential about what it means to be a teenage girl—how their emotions refuse to arrive one at a time.

In adolescence, joy doesn't cancel out sadness. Excitement doesn't erase anxiety. Anger, shame, fear, happiness—they all live inside her at once, sometimes overlapping, sometimes contradicting, often exhausting her from the inside out.

As adults, we've learned to file our emotions into neat boxes. We separate logic from feeling. We say things like, *"I shouldn't feel this way,"* or *"I'll deal with that later."* But our daughters? They feel everything now, all at once, with no manual to tell them what it means or how to sort it.

There were days Kalpana would come home from school with a smile, talk about something funny that happened and then suddenly go quiet. A small comment from a friend, a mistake on a test, an uncomfortable moment—it would all come crashing down later, disguised as an argument at the dinner table or a slammed door.

It used to confuse me. I'd wonder, what just happened? She was fine a minute ago. But she wasn't fine. She was layered.

And the truth is: I was the one who needed to stop chasing stability in her. I needed to stop holding her to some version of **"emotional normal"** that didn't match the reality of what she was going through.

Once I stopped trying to fix the contradictions—once I stopped saying things like, *"But you were happy earlier,"* or *"Why are you crying now?"*—I began to understand her more.

I began to meet her where she was, even if where she was didn't make perfect sense. And what she needed from me was not analysis. Not correction. Not even comfort, always. What she needed was permission to feel without needing to justify it.

So now, when I see her laugh and cry in the same breath, I don't interrupt. I don't ask her to pick a side—happy or sad. I just sit beside her, hold the space steady and remind myself: She's not broken. She's just becoming.

Teaching Emotional Honesty, Not Perfection

There was a time I believed that part of my job as a mother was to teach Kalpana how to "control" her emotions. To guide her into maturity by helping her respond calmly, to be rational, to not cry over small things or shout when overwhelmed. I thought I was showing her how to be strong.

But I've slowly come to understand emotional strength doesn't mean hiding your feelings. It means being able to name them, sit with them and share them—without shame.

Kalpana doesn't need me to be a model of emotional perfection. She needs to see what emotional honesty looks like in real life.

So, I've stopped holding her to impossible standards, especially when she's upset. I no longer say things like *"Be mature"* or *"Handle this better."* Instead, I remind myself that she is still learning—and that her emotional outbursts aren't failures. They're signs that she's processing, feeling, experiencing. They're evidence of growth, not weakness.

But it wasn't enough to just give her room to feel.

I realised I had to show her what that looks like. Not by telling her what to feel, but by showing her what I feel. Genuinely. Without trying to **"keep it together"** all the time.

So now, when I feel anxious before a meeting, I say it out loud.

When a friend or colleague makes me feel ignored or dismissed, I don't bottle it up. I share it in simple words. When I miss her after a long day of silence between us, I don't hide behind chores or distractions. I just say it: *"I missed you today."*

What surprised me was how gently she began to mirror that honesty. Not dramatically. Not always through conversation. But through little truths shared more often. Those moments—**however fleeting**—are the real signs of emotional maturity. Not perfection. Not control. Just honesty.

We've created something in our home now that I never had growing up—a culture of feeling. A space where emotions aren't treated as weaknesses or problems to solve, but as parts of being human.

She's learning that she doesn't need to be happy all the time. She doesn't need to impress anyone with how **"strong"** she is. She can just be real.

And I? I'm learning too. That parenting is less about shaping her into someone else—and more about meeting her exactly as she is, over and over again, until she feels safe to keep showing up that way.

From Mood Swings to Meaning

There was a time when every sudden outburst from Kalpana felt like a crisis. A slammed door would echo like rejection. A moody silence at dinner felt like failure. Her unpredictability left me walking on eggshells, unsure whether I was doing too much—or not enough.

One day she'd be laughing and helping me with the cooking and the next, she wouldn't come out of her room. One morning, she'd hug me before school and that same evening, she'd tell me to leave her alone.

It used to leave me confused. Worried. Even hurt. I would respond with urgency—pushing, questioning, offering advice too soon or too much.

But slowly, as I've watched her grow, I've learned something important: Mood swings aren't manipulation. They're communication and even when she says, *"I don't want to talk about it,"* what she's really saying is: *"I don't know how to explain it yet."*

These days, things still get stormy. There are still eye rolls and heavy sighs. There are still moments when she disappears behind her headphones and avoids conversation altogether.

But now, every so often, she surprises me. She'll pause in the middle of her own frustration and say, *"I think I'm just overwhelmed."*

Not with perfect calm. Not like a therapist in training. But with effort. With honesty. And in those small words, I see something big: progress.

Not just for her—for me, too. Because now, when she's crying, I don't panic. I don't rush in with tissues and reasons why she shouldn't feel the way she does.

I simply sit beside her. I reach for her hand. and I say, *"It's okay to feel everything."* That one sentence has become my anchor—our anchor. This is the shift I never knew I needed to make—not just in parenting, but in how I love.

To stop measuring progress by how **"stable"** or **"cheerful"** she is and instead to recognise that real growth means she now feels safe enough to name what she's going through. Even if it's messy. Especially if it is.

Because feeling, expressing and healing are not separate stages. They live side by side, feeding each other.

And every time I choose presence over panic, every time I sit without solving—I teach her that it's safe to feel. To feel everything.

That's where the meaning is. Inside the mood swing, not beyond it.

Chapter 5
From Meltdowns to Meaning

Kalpana stood in the middle of the hallway, on the verge of tears—because I had worn her earrings.

She was getting ready for her friend's birthday party and came into my room to ask for her silver hoops, the ones she had bought with her first ever pocket money. That's when she saw them—dangling from my ears, already matched with my outfit and worn without her knowing.

"You wore my earrings?" she asked, her voice rising. *"Without even asking me?"*

I blinked. *"I just borrowed them for the evening, beta. I thought you wouldn't mind."* That's all I said. Calmly. Honestly.

But her eyes filled instantly. Her face turned red. She stormed into her room, shouting, *"Why does nobody in this house respect my stuff?"*

And then the door slammed shut.

At first, I was stunned. They were just earrings. I had worn them before. I always kept them back. Why such a reaction? But something in her voice—something tight and heavy—told me this wasn't about earrings at all.

Later that evening, while she was still locked in her room and the rest of us were getting ready for a marriage function, I wrote her a short message on a sticky note and left it on her table: *"I'm sorry I wore your earrings without asking. I should've respected they're yours. I'm here if you want to talk."*

She didn't come out for dinner. She didn't go to the party. But the next morning, as I was making breakfast, she came and stood quietly at the door.

"I just… feel like nothing is mine anymore," she said. *"Everyone takes my stuff, tells me what to wear, how to behave. That one pair of earrings — it just felt like at least that was mine."*

And in that moment, I finally understood. Her meltdown wasn't about silver hoops. It was about ownership. Boundaries. Identity. Control. All the things teenagers are trying to build as they grow. She wasn't being dramatic — she was trying to claim a space for herself and I had unknowingly stepped on it.

Over time, I've started seeing these outbursts differently. I don't react to the tone, the volume, the door slams. I listen for what's underneath.

When Kalpana says, *"You never get it!"* she often means, *"I don't know how to explain this and it's scary."* When she walks away mid-sentence, it's usually, *"I feel too full. I need space before I break."* These moments are not about disobedience. They're about emotional overload.

I've learned that not every tantrum needs a response. Some just need patience. Some need silence. Some need a cup of tea left quietly outside her door. Some just need time. Once I stopped seeing her reactions as problems to fix and started seeing them as feelings to honour, things slowly shifted. And in learning to speak her own emotional language, she was learning something I couldn't teach her through advice — self-awareness.

One night, weeks after the earring incident, we were sitting on the balcony. She looked at me and said softly, *"I know I overreacted that day. But it really did matter to me."* I nodded and smiled. *"I get it now. It wasn't just about the earrings."*

She gave a half-smile and said, *"Thanks for not yelling. It made me want to come talk."* And that's when I knew we were making progress.

Because the truth is—tantrums are not a failure of parenting. They're a part of growing. They're our daughters asking: *"Can you love me even when I'm a mess?"* And if we listen closely enough, we'll realise— they're not pushing us away. They're hoping we'll stay close… just in quieter, more patient ways.

What Tantrums Actually Are

Tantrums. The word alone can make a parent feel exhausted. We tend to associate them with toddlers in grocery store aisles, red-faced and rolling on the floor because they didn't get a chocolate bar. But teenage tantrums? They look different. They don't always involve screaming or tears. Sometimes they're quiet, icy, sharp-tongued or withdrawn. And more than anything, they confuse us.

As parents, it's easy to label them: drama, attitude, disrespect. We think, *"Why can't she just talk like a normal person?"* or *"This is unnecessary—what's the big deal?"* But what we often miss is that these outbursts aren't calculated or malicious. They're unspoken messages.

A tantrum is what happens when too many emotions get crammed into a space that hasn't yet learned how to hold them. It's not about bad behaviour—it's about emotional overload. Teenagers, much like toddlers, still lack the tools to name and regulate their big feelings. And when those feelings have nowhere to go, they burst through the cracks—in loud, confusing, sometimes hurtful ways.

Your daughter might not know how to say, *"I'm overwhelmed."* She might not know how to admit, *"I'm scared to fail,"* or *"I'm feeling invisible today."*

So instead, she might raise her voice. Slam a door. Snap at you when all you did was ask about her day. Underneath all that? It's not ego. It's not rebellion. It's pain. It's stress. It's sadness. It's a brain and body that are developing at different speeds, trying to communicate emotions it doesn't yet fully understand.

And while it's hard—really hard—not to react with our own anger or frustration, it helps to pause and ask ourselves:

What is she really trying to say?

Over time, I've learned that when Kalpana lashes out or shuts down, it's not about disrespect. It's a signal. An emotional fire alarm. A flare being sent up, saying, *"Something inside me doesn't feel okay and I don't know how to ask for help."*

And when I choose to stay calm, to not mirror the tantrum with my own emotional fire, something beautiful happens. She eventually softens. The storm passes. And what's left is a girl who just needed to feel safe enough to come undone—and still be loved.

So no, tantrums aren't just noise. They're not disobedience or defiance. They are the unfiltered voice of a heart learning how to speak.

And the more we listen—really listen—the less they feel like battles and the more they become bridges. Bridges to understanding. Bridges to connection. Bridges to healing.

The "Outburst" Before our Haridwar Trip

It was meant to be a break. A quiet, spiritual reset in Haridwar. I had imagined everything—early morning aartis by the Ganga, peaceful temple visits, a chance for all of us to step away from our screens, our stress, our pace. Especially Kalpana, who I thought could use the stillness the most.

But the night before we were supposed to leave, the house felt anything but peaceful. I had reminded her—gently, I thought—to pack a few simple outfits, something respectful for the temples. And that's when it all cracked open.

"Why do you always treat me like a baby?" she shouted. *"You just want me to act like some perfect Sanskari girl for relatives!"* She was loud, upset, flustered—and in that moment, I felt completely blindsided. I was hurt. Angry, even. My first instinct was to tell her how ungrateful she sounded. I wanted to say, "We're doing this for you!"

But something in her face stopped me. Behind the fire in her eyes, I saw something more fragile: **exhaustion.**

She stormed into her room and slammed the door. I stayed in the kitchen longer than I needed to, stirring tea I didn't even drink. My mind was racing—how did a family trip become a battleground?

Later that night, I walked into her room. She was lying on her bed, earbuds in, staring at the ceiling. I didn't speak at first. I just sat quietly.

After a few minutes, she said—barely above a whisper—*"I'm tired, Mumma. Not just school-tired. I don't know how to explain it."*

I nodded. I didn't push. I didn't fix. I just placed my hand gently on hers and said, *"You don't have to come if you don't want to. But if you do, we'll go slow. You can be quiet. You don't have to smile for anyone."*

There was no big emotional moment. No hug. No sorry. But something shifted. The next morning, she came to the dining table with her small grey backpack and said, *"I packed. I'll come. Just… don't expect me to talk too much."* I smiled and simply replied, *"Okay."*

And on the way to Haridwar, she sat next to the window, headphones in, not saying much—but she was there. With us. Choosing to come, in her own way, on her own terms. That evening, as the lamps floated on the river during the Ganga aarti, I saw her watching quietly— eyes soft, posture relaxed, not resisting anymore. Not pretending either. Just being.

And in that moment, I realised: she didn't need to be excited, cheerful or *"on her best behaviour"* to belong. She needed space. Choice. Respect. She needed to be allowed to enter gently, without performance. Her outburst wasn't about the trip—it was about needing to feel heard before being asked to show up. And once she felt that, she came—not because she had to, but because she wanted to. That, to me, is real growth. For her. And for me.

The Volcano Analogy

One evening, after yet another emotional outburst that came seemingly out of nowhere, I sat with Kalpana in her room. The anger had passed, but the tension still lingered in the air like smoke after a fire. I wanted to explain something without sounding like I was lecturing her. So, I took a deep breath and said, *"You know, your emotions remind me of a volcano."*

She gave me a sceptical look, but I continued. *"When you bottle things up—your frustration, your sadness, your stress—it's like magma building under the surface. It stays there, hidden, heating up. And then one day, when you can't hold it in anymore… BOOM. It explodes."*

To my surprise, she smiled. A small, real smile. *"Like Mount Vesuvius (an active volcano in southern Italy)?"* she asked, half-teasing. I laughed and said, *"Exactly. You're my personal Vesuvius."* It became a turning point—not because the metaphor magically changed everything but because it gave us a shared language. Something simple, visual and true.

Since then, we've started to use the volcano as a way to check in. Not every day. Not always successfully. But often enough to make a difference. Now, instead of waiting for the eruption, she sometimes gives me signals—little moments of honesty that weren't there before. She'll say things like: *"I'm not in the mood today." "Can I just be alone for a bit?" "I don't want to talk but can you sit in the room?"*

Tiny phrases. Easily overlooked. But to me, they're seismic shifts. Because they mean she's trying to let the pressure out before it builds too high. And more than that, it means she trusts me enough to let me in before the explosion.

Of course, it's not always smooth. There are still eruptions—slammed doors, sharp words, tears that come out of nowhere. But now, they feel less scary. Less like chaos and more like weather. Predictable in their unpredictability.

And slowly, we're learning to manage the emotional climate together. She's learning that she doesn't have to hold it all in. That she can release the steam in small, safe ways. And I'm learning that my role isn't to cap the volcano—it's to stand nearby, steady and safe, so she knows she doesn't have to erupt alone.

Because underneath that volcano is a girl who feels deeply. Who doesn't always have the words but always has the need to be heard. And when we meet her fire with patience, not fear, we stop dreading the blast and start building a bridge—across lava, across silence, across whatever comes next.

What Worked (And What Didn't)

There's no manual for raising a teenage girl. No step-by-step guide that tells you how to respond when your once-chatty daughter turns into a wall of silence or when the smallest request sparks a full-blown meltdown. I tried a lot of things—some well-meaning, some desperate. And over time, I started to see patterns. Things that pushed her further away. Things that gently brought her back.

Let's start with what didn't work

Lectures during meltdowns were the worst. In those heated moments, when she was already overwhelmed, my long explanations about *"respect"* or *"how lucky she is"* landed like noise. If anything, they made her feel more cornered, more misunderstood. She'd shut down or argue harder and we'd both end up exhausted, neither of us heard.

Then there was the classic:

"Calm down." I said it more times than I can count. And every time I said it, she got louder. Angrier. More hurt. I thought I was helping—

asking her to find peace. But what she heard was, *"Stop feeling the way you feel."* And of course, that only made things worse.

And let's not forget the threats—the heat-of-the-moment punishments like, *"That's it, you're grounded!"* They weren't planned or productive. They came from my own panic. And in hindsight, they never worked. They didn't teach her anything except how unpredictable my love could feel when she was at her worst.

But slowly, through experience, I discovered what actually helped.

Staying calm myself—even when I had to fake it— made all the difference. When I kept my voice steady, even while her volume was rising, it brought something down in the room. She didn't always notice it right away, but over time, she began to match my energy. Even if she didn't calm down immediately, the fight didn't spiral the way it used to.

Saying things like, *"Let's take a break and talk when we're both less angry,"* gave us both permissions to cool off without guilt. It wasn't avoidance. It was strategy. It gave her time to sort her feelings without feeling punished or dismissed.

And the most powerful tool I found? Asking her later—not during, but after— *"What were you feeling under all that shouting?"* Sometimes she didn't have an answer. Sometimes she shrugged. But occasionally, a quiet truth would tumble out. A glimpse into the heart behind the outburst.

One day, after one of the loudest fights we'd had in weeks, she quietly walked into the room while I was folding laundry. No drama. No announcement. Just a girl who had come through something. She sat beside me and said, *"Mumma, I wasn't mad at you. I just had a horrible day."*

And that one sentence made it all worth it.

All the restraint. All the deep breaths. All the moments where I held back from fixing or fighting. Because when she said that, I knew she trusted me with the real story, not just the emotional explosion. And that trust—fragile, hard-won and priceless—is what I had been working for all along.

The Meltdown as a Message

Listening to what her emotions are really trying to say. It took me a long time to realise that not every meltdown was about the moment in front of me. At first, I'd see the shouting, the eye-rolls, the sudden storm of tears as overreaction—or worse, disrespect. I'd react defensively, correcting her tone or lecturing her about gratitude. I took it personally, every single time.

But slowly, quietly, something shifted. I started paying attention to the patterns. The timing. The tension that built before the outburst. And I began to see something that changed everything: Her meltdowns weren't just about what I said. They were messages. Messages she didn't yet know how to say out loud. Messages she didn't even always understand herself.

Sometimes a tantrum said: "I feel unseen." "I'm drowning in pressure." "I miss the old version of me." "I need help, but I don't want to be a burden."

She didn't say those words, of course. Not directly. Instead, she'd yell because I reminded her about her homework. Or cry when I asked her to come downstairs for dinner. Or get angry when I suggested we go for a walk.

But beneath every explosion was something deeper. Something human. Something real. And when I reminded myself of that—when I made space to see the feeling behind the reaction—I could shift from fighting her to understanding her. Not perfectly. Not every time. I still lose my cool. I still raise my voice. I still sometimes forget to breathe before I speak. But more and more, I'm learning to pause.

To ask myself: *What is she trying to say underneath all this?*

It's rarely about what triggered her. It's about everything that's built up—school, friends, hormones, identity, pressure to perform, to belong to "be okay." It's about needing someone to hold all of that with her, not shrink it down or push it away.

And when I can remember that—when I can listen, not to the volume, but to the ache behind it—something opens between us. She calms down faster. I feel less lost. And trust starts to build in the quiet after the storm. Because what looks like defiance is often just a girl trying to be heard—not through words, but through emotion.

And if I can hear her, really hear her, she doesn't need to shout quite so loud next time.

Choosing Connection Over Control

Every parent wants a well-behaved child. We want calm dinners, respectful responses, neatly folded feelings. We hope for politeness and poise, especially when the world is watching. And when that doesn't happen—when our daughters yell, cry, slam doors or go silent—it's easy to panic. Easy to think, where did I go wrong?

For the longest time, I believed that emotional outbursts were signs of failure—hers or mine. I believed that I had to **"fix"** her behaviour quickly. That I had to remind her who was in charge. That I had to stay one step ahead, always.

But slowly and sometimes painfully, I've learned: control may bring silence, but it doesn't build trust. Control demands obedience. Connection offers understanding. And when I started choosing connection over control, everything changed. Now, instead of saying *"Enough! Stop crying over nothing!"*, I try saying, *"That seemed really hard. Want to talk about it?"*

Instead of *"Don't talk to me like that,"* I take a breath and offer, *"It's okay to feel big things. I'm still here."* Because behind every sharp word and slammed door, what she's really asking is: *"Can you still love me— even like this?"* That's the part that broke me open.

Her anger, her resistance, even her silence—they weren't rejection. They were the messy, emotional language of a girl still learning how to be human in a body full of hormones and a mind full of confusion.

And every time I chose presence over punishment, warmth over warnings, patience over panic—I saw a little more trust grow between us.

Not perfectly. Not instantly. But quietly. Steadily.

Connection doesn't mean permissiveness. It doesn't mean letting go of boundaries. It means letting go of the illusion that being in control is the same as being in relationship. It means showing up even when it's inconvenient. It means sitting beside her even when she's pushing me away. It means understanding that her worst moments aren't tests of my authority—they're invitations to love her harder.

And slowly, with that kind of love, she's learning something powerful:

That she doesn't have to scream to be heard. That she doesn't have to hide her emotions to be accepted. That connection isn't earned through perfection—it's offered through grace.

And that's the kind of strength I want her to carry into the world.

Chapter 6

The Power of the Pause

It was one of those mornings when everything was moving too fast. The school bus was waiting downstairs, Kalpana had forgotten to pack her bag and her uniform skirt had a mysterious ketchup stain from the day before. I was already irritated. I hadn't even had morning tea and my phone was buzzing with work messages.

In the middle of the chaos, I asked her to tie her hair. For the third time. She looked up, frustrated and snapped, *"Can you stop nagging me? I'm not a baby!"* And for a moment, I almost snapped back. I could feel the anger rising up in my throat, the familiar heat in my cheeks. The words were right there— *"Don't you dare speak to me like that!"* —waiting to fire.

But something inside me said: wait. Just pause. So, I took a breath. I turned off the gas and I didn't say anything. Kalpana stormed out, tied her hair in the hallway, grabbed her bag and left with barely a goodbye. The door shut behind her with a soft thud that felt louder than it actually was.

I stood there in the kitchen, tea still untouched and just… breathed. That pause changed everything. Because if I had reacted—if I had shouted back, made it about her tone, demanded respect in that moment—I know exactly what would've followed: anger, silence, guilt, distance.

Instead, I gave her space. Not as a reward, but as an offering. Space to feel what she was feeling. Space to realise she had spoken harshly. Space to come back when she was ready.

That evening, around 6 p.m., she came into the kitchen quietly while I was making dinner. She didn't say sorry right away. She just stood beside me and said, *"I was having a rough morning."* I nodded. *"I figured."* Then she added, *"Thanks for not yelling."*

That's all it took. Not a long conversation. Not a dramatic apology. Just a moment of connection—built because I paused instead of reacting.

It hasn't always been like this. There were so many times in the past when I let my emotions take over. When I shouted because I felt disrespected. When I cried because I felt helpless. When I said things like, *"You don't value anything I do,"* just because I was tired.

But every time I matched her volume, I lost something. A little bit of trust. A little bit of closeness. A little piece of the safe space I was trying so hard to create.

I realised that Kalpana didn't need a perfect mother—she needed a steady one. Not someone who never got upset, but someone who knew when to step back instead of step in. Now, when I feel my patience thinning, I ask myself one question:

"Is this the moment I teach her fear—or safety?"

Because when we pause, we don't just avoid conflict—we open space for connection. And in that space, she feels safe enough to come back. To speak. To reflect. To grow. I've learned that silence can be healing. That not every action needs a reaction. That calm doesn't mean weakness—it means wisdom.

Kalpana is still learning how to manage her storms. But I'm learning how to be her calm. Not by fixing her moods. Not by controlling every situation. Just by standing still long enough for her to know I'm not going anywhere.

Why Pausing Works

There's something in us, as mothers, that makes us want to jump in. Fix the problem. Defend our point. Calm the chaos. When our daughters are angry, rude or overwhelmed, we feel this urgency—to be heard, to explain, to solve. It comes from love, of course. From wanting things to be okay again. From wanting them to understand that we're not the enemy.

But here's the truth I've learned—in those heated moments, nothing we say actually lands. Not the logic. Not the reminders. Not the wisdom. Because in that moment, they're flooded. Flooded with hormones that blur judgment. With school stress they don't know how to talk about. With friendship tensions, body changes and big emotions that don't yet have names.

And when we react—when we raise our voice, lecture or punish— it's like throwing gasoline on a spark. But when we pause, even for a few seconds, something shifts. Not in them—at first—but in us.

That pause is small, but sacred. It creates a gap between stimulus and response, between her chaos and our reaction. It's in that tiny space that something more powerful than control is born compassion. That pause says more than words can. It says:

"I'm not here to overpower you."
"I see that you're hurting, even if I don't understand it yet."
"I'm choosing relationship over reaction."
"We're on the same side."

And when I've taken that pause—even when my blood was boiling—it has changed everything. It's not magic. It doesn't instantly end the meltdown or fix the problem. But it keeps the door open. It keeps the room safe. It tells her: You're allowed to feel messy here—and I'm strong enough to hold it without adding more noise.

Over time, I've noticed something beautiful. The more I pause, the more she softens. Maybe not in the moment—but later. She returns. She reflects. Sometimes she even says, *"I was really upset. I didn't mean what I said."*

And I know then that my silence wasn't weakness. It was wisdom. Because what looks like doing nothing is actually doing the hardest thing of all: Staying grounded when everything else is spinning. That's why pausing works. Not to win. Not to be right. But to stay in connection with a daughter who's still learning how to come back to herself—and needs to know we'll be here when she does.

The Birthday That Didn't Feel Special

Kalpana had been quiet all evening on her birthday. Not angry. Not sad exactly. Just… distant. She'd smiled when the cake came out. She said thank you when the gifts were handed over. She posed for photos. But I could tell—something was missing. Her laughter didn't reach her eyes.

Later that night, when everyone had left and the house was quiet, I walked into her room and asked, *"Did you enjoy today?"* She shrugged. *"Yeah, it was fine."* Fine. That word again. I sat on the edge of her bed, unsure whether to push. Then I said, *"You just didn't seem very happy."*

She stared at the ceiling and after a long pause, said, *"It just felt like no one really saw me."* My heart dropped. I thought I had done everything right—planned her favourite cake, invited the people she liked, decorated with her favourite colours. But I realized I had focused on the outside of the celebration. She was longing for something quieter, something more meaningful: to feel understood, not just celebrated.

I wanted to say, *"But we did so much for you!"* But I stopped myself. That wasn't what she needed. So, I said instead, *"Tell me what you wish today had felt like."*

And she did. She talked about how she wanted to go for a walk alone that morning but the day had been too packed. How she missed her old friend but didn't know how to say that during cake cutting. How she felt weird wearing the outfit I picked when she wanted to wear her oversized hoodie instead.

They were little things—but they mattered. That night, I didn't fix it. I didn't try to make her feel guilty for not feeling grateful. I just listened. And that changed everything.

Because sometimes, what our daughters need most on special days is not the celebration—it's connection. That birthday reminded me: presence is the real present. And listening, without judgment or defence is the most generous thing we can offer.

Not Every Moment Needs a Response

There was a stretch of weeks—maybe months—when every interaction with Kalpana felt like walking into a sarcastic windstorm. She had perfected the art of the eye roll.

I would ask the most harmless question—*"Did you pack your lunch?"*—and her eyes would shoot to the ceiling like I'd just insulted her intelligence. If I complimented her outfit or simply asked how school went, the response was the same: irritation masked in silence, layered with a dramatic sigh or that now-familiar upward glance. At first, I took every single one of those moments to heart. I felt disrespected. Dismissed. Invisible in my own home.

My instinct, like any parent, was to react. To correct. To lecture. I wanted her to understand that tone and respect matter. That I deserved better. But the more I pushed back, the more she hardened. It became a loop: I asked. She rolled her eyes. I called it out. She stormed away. And I was left in the kitchen, angry and confused, wondering how we'd gone from bedtime stories to emotional minefields.

One afternoon, after a particularly tense breakfast, I realized that I wasn't just responding to her—I was trying to control her emotions through my reactions. Her attitude triggered something in me that had little to do with her. It was about being seen. Being heard. Being valued.

And in trying to demand respect, I was missing the real opportunity: to teach calm, not command it.

So, I made a conscious shift. The next time she gave me the look, I didn't raise my voice. I didn't sigh louder. I didn't meet her sarcasm with my own. I simply nodded and carried on. I chose stillness, not silence. Intention, not withdrawal. And that pause—small and unspectacular on the surface—began to change everything.

At first, she was visibly thrown. She waited for me to bite back, to correct her tone, to start the same old argument. But I didn't. And without my reaction to feed her defiance, something softened. Not instantly. Not dramatically. But slowly, in the way ice starts to melt—not with a crack, but with a quiet shift in temperature.

By not rising to meet her mood, I was offering her something much more powerful than authority—I was offering her emotional space. The space to not get it right every time. The space to come back to herself without guilt. And the space for me to see the bigger picture. That behind the eye rolls and short replies was often a tired, overwhelmed, overstimulated girl who just didn't have the energy to fake politeness.

It's tempting, always, to address behaviour in the moment. To hold the line. To assert ourselves as parents. But sometimes, growth doesn't come from confrontation—it comes from a calm that says: *"I'm not here to fight you. I'm here to stay with you, even when you're hard to love."*

Now, the eye rolls haven't disappeared. But they don't sting the same way. Because I've stopped expecting emotional perfection. I've started seeing those little moments not as attacks, but as signals. Indicators of her inner state, not judgments of mine. And in doing so, I've given both of us permission to breathe.

So, no—every moment doesn't need a response. Sometimes, the strongest parenting move is the quiet one. The one that doesn't demand respect but models it. The one that says: I'm here. I'm listening. And I choose connection over control—even when it's hard.

The Pause Is Not Weakness

There's an idea that lives in many of our homes—passed down from parents and elders like old advice. It's not always spoken directly, but we've all heard versions of its growing up:

"Bachchon ko control mein rakho."
"If you don't respond right away, they'll walk all over you."
"Answer back ka matlab hai badtameezi. Bad parenting."

I grew up around that mindset—the idea that silence means surrender, that softness equals permissiveness. So, when Kalpana became a teenager, my instincts kicked in fast. Every time she snapped, rolled her eyes or questioned my instructions, my body tensed. I felt a surge of pressure—not just to respond, but to correct her, to show strength, to reclaim my authority.

But here's the truth I've had to learn—and unlearn: **Pausing isn't weakness. It's wisdom.**

When our kids are emotional—when they're shouting, shutting down or arguing—they're not in a space where they can hear logic or even love. Their brains are in fight-or-flight mode. Words bounce off. Tone takes over. If we jump in with the same energy, we're not teaching anything but escalation.

I used to believe that pausing meant I was losing ground. That if I didn't assert my *"final word,"* I was giving Kalpana too much power. But over time, I've seen the opposite happen. When I stay calm—even when I'm boiling inside—it sets the tone. It breaks the cycle.

She expects me to react. But when I don't—when I take a breath, meet her chaos with calm—something shifts. Not always immediately. But over time, she begins to mirror it. Not because I demanded respect but because I showed her how to offer it.

The pause isn't about ignoring bad behaviour. It's not permission to be rude or dismissive. It's about choosing the right moment to respond. It's about waiting until the storm has passed so our words can actually reach their hearts.

I've noticed that when I respond after the pause, my voice is steadier. My words are kinder. My intentions are clearer. And instead of a shouting match, what follows is usually a conversation.

This isn't passive parenting. It's intentional parenting. And it's hard. It takes discipline. Strength. The kind of strength our culture doesn't always see or name.

But I see it now. And I feel it every time Kalpana comes back later and says, *"I didn't mean to talk like that."* Or, *"Thanks for not shouting back."*

So no, pausing is not weakness. It's clarity. It's emotional courage. It's choosing peace when everything in you wants to push back. And that kind of parenting may not always look loud or traditional. But it builds trust. It builds respect. And it teaches our daughters what real strength looks like—quiet, grounded and full of grace.

My Favourite Line

Parenting a teenager often feels like walking a tightrope—with your heart in one hand and your patience in the other. There are moments when emotions run high, voices rise and the urge to correct, explain or react bubbles to the surface. I've been there more times than I can count—standing in the hallway outside Kalpana's room, feeling frustrated, helpless and desperate for her to just talk to me.

And while I believed I was teaching boundaries, what I was actually doing was adding pressure to an already overwhelmed mind. I wanted to resolve things immediately—but she needed space. She needed silence. She needed permission to come down from the storm without fear of more thunder waiting outside her door.

So, I started saying something different. Something softer. Something that changed everything. Now, when Kalpana is upset—

really upset—I take a breath, step back and say: *"I'm here. We'll talk when you're ready."*

That's it. No demand. No emotional tug. Just quiet reassurance. At first, she didn't respond. Sometimes she rolled her eyes. Sometimes she closed the door.

But then—something shifted. She began coming back. Not always right away. Not dramatically. But in small ways that meant everything.

A tap on the shoulder while I was in the kitchen. A quiet *"Can we talk?"* before bedtime. A late-night confession that had been building for days. Because what that sentence told her—without needing a lecture—was this: You are still safe here. Even when you're angry. Even when you're distant. Even when you've said hurtful things.

The pause between conflict and conversation became a doorway instead of a wall. And now, it's my favourite line. Not because it solves everything instantly. But because it creates space for healing instead of hardening. Because it shifts the energy from confrontation to comfort. Because it lets her know that no matter how stormy her emotions get, my love is still steady.

So, the next time your daughter walks away in anger or shuts you out in silence, try it. Then wait. You might be surprised at what returns through that open door.

The Power of the Pause, In Practice

Pausing sounds like a simple idea—just wait before reacting. But in the middle of an emotional storm, it's anything but easy. When your daughter raises her voice, rolls her eyes or walks away mid-sentence, your body tightens. Your mind screams: Say something! It takes everything in you not to respond from that place of heat. But that pause? That deliberate breath before the reply. That's where the magic lives.

I've had to teach myself this over and over again. Not in theory—but in practice. And practice, as the word suggests, means I still mess up. I still lose my cool. I still raise my voice when I wish I hadn't. But more often now, I catch myself.

These days, I try to start with a breath. Just one. Deep, intentional, slow. It's my way of telling my nervous system: You're safe. You don't have to match her mood. You can choose calm. Then I remind myself: She's not attacking you. She's overwhelmed. She doesn't have the words, so she's showing you the feelings instead.

If I feel like I'm about to say something, I'll regret—something sharp or sarcastic—I walk away. Not to shut her out. Not to punish her. But to protect both of us from words that are hard to take back. That space, even if it's just a few minutes in the next room, gives me a moment to reset.

And when I come back—when we both do—it's different. She's quieter. I'm clearer. The air is softer. We're no longer in survival mode and now there's room for listening. Sometimes we talk. Sometimes we just sit. But the tension fades not because I won the argument—but because I didn't feed it. Is it perfect? No. Parenting never is. Some days, the pause feels like a struggle. Some days, I forget it altogether and say the wrong thing at the wrong time. But slowly, I'm learning. And Kalpana is too.

Because what started as me pausing for her has become something we're learning to do together. She notices now when I don't react. She softens when I hold space instead of snapping. And I see her pausing too—catching herself mid-eyeroll, mid-snap and choosing differently.

This small habit has changed the rhythm of our home. There's less shouting. Less slamming of doors. More circling back. More repairing. More quiet moments where love sits in the space between the words.

The pause isn't passive. It's powerful. It's a choice to stop the emotional dominoes from falling. And in that space, something else grows: trust, safety and the kind of relationship that doesn't just survive teenagerhood—but deepens through it.

What She's Learning Too

It was a simple ordinary moment—one of those domestic scenes that doesn't ask for attention. Kalpana and I were standing in the bedroom folding laundry. T-shirts, towels, bedsheets. No big conversation. No drama. Just the soft rustle of cotton and the kind of silence that feels companionable. She looked over at me mid-fold and said,

"You're different now. You don't yell like before."

I stopped, holding one of her kurtas in my hands. I turned toward her, smiled and said, *"You're different too."* She nodded, thoughtful. Then, with that quiet maturity that sometimes catches me off guard, she said, *"I think we both needed space to figure each other out."*

I didn't respond right away. I just held that moment in my heart—because it was more than words. It was a reflection. A mirror. Proof that everything we'd been trying to build—every pause, every hard conversation, every held breath—was taking root. Not just in me, but in her too.

For a long time, I thought parenting was a one-way street. That I had to teach, shape, guide. That she would grow and I would stay steady. But the truth is, we're both growing at the same time. She's figuring out how to be a teenager, how to name her feelings, how to find her voice. And I'm figuring out how to be her mother through this version of her—this changing, blossoming, beautiful mess of contradictions.

The more I've learned to pause, the more I've seen her doing it too. Fewer storms, fewer slammed doors. More quiet returns. More moments like this one, folding laundry and naming what had changed—not just between us, but within us.

And that's the part no one really talks about: when we model emotional growth, they start practicing it too. Not perfectly. Not all at once. But gently. Gradually. The pause didn't just give me time to calm down. It gave her time to breathe. To realise that she didn't have to defend herself all the time. That our home wasn't a battleground, but a place she could come undone and still be held.

We came back to each other; with less noise and more kindness.

Chapter 7

Mirror: The Role of Self-Image

Kalpana stood in front of the mirror far longer than usual that evening. She had changed outfits three times already. I heard the rustling from the other room; a kurta thrown on the bed, then a top tossed to the floor, then the creak of her wardrobe opening again. I didn't say anything. But I could feel her frustration from a distance.

When she finally came out, she was wearing a loose t-shirt over jeans, hair tied back, lips pressed into a straight line. *"You look nice,"* I said gently. She didn't even look up. *"It's fine,"* she replied. *"Can we just go?"*

Later, when we got back from dinner at her cousin's place, she didn't speak much. She ate quietly, scrolled through her phone and disappeared into her room without the usual *"good night."* I followed her after a few minutes and found her lying on her bed, face half-buried in her pillow, screen lighting up her face in the dark.

"Everything okay?" I asked, sitting beside her. She shrugged. *"Everyone just looks so... perfect. Their skin, their hair, their outfits. And I ...."* she paused, then whispered, *"I hate how I look in everything."*

That moment broke me a little. Because here was my daughter; my bright, beautiful, funny Kalpana; so unsure of herself, because of things she saw on a screen. The same girl who used to wear mismatched socks proudly and call herself a "fashion queen" now couldn't look at herself without comparison.

I didn't want to lie to her. I didn't say, *"You're prettier than all of them."* I knew that wouldn't land. Instead, I asked, *"Do you want to talk about what changed? You never used to feel this way."* She hesitated, then said, *"I don't know. It's just… you scroll and scroll and everyone looks happy and perfect. And you start to feel like you're the only one who doesn't."*

Social media had become her mirror; and it was a cruel one. It didn't reflect her spirit, her kindness, her humour or her creativity. It only reflected angles and filters and poses and edits. And the saddest part? She believed it.

She believed her worth was tied to what she saw on someone else's curated feed. So, I tried something different. Over the next few days, I started talking about my own insecurities. About how I used to compare my body to my cousins'. About how I once avoided sarees because I didn't like my arms. About the years I wasted trying to look like someone else, before finally feeling okay as myself.

And Kalpana listened. Not because she suddenly felt better, but because she realised; she wasn't the only one. This wasn't just her private failure. It was something so many girls, women and mothers go through. Quietly. Repeatedly.

I didn't ban her from social media. I didn't give a lecture about "real beauty." I just started showing her small truths. I reminded her of who she is without the mirror. How she helped her friend through a panic attack last week. How her younger brother copies her dance moves. How she makes the whole family laugh with just one raised eyebrow.

Bit by bit, I reminded her that her value doesn't shrink or grow based on how tight her jeans feel on any given day. And slowly, something shifted. Not perfectly. Not overnight. But I noticed her spending more time reading again. Singing again. Wearing bright colours again. Complaining less about her face. Laughing more freely. Leaving the house without checking herself five times in the mirror.

She even said once, softly, *"I'm starting to like how I look in yellow."* It was such a small line. But for me, it felt like the beginning of healing. Our daughters don't need us to tell them they're beautiful. They need us to show them that they are whole. With breakouts. With bloated tummies. With untamed hair. With feelings that are too big and mirrors that are too cruel.

They need us to help them find their confidence outside the mirror; so that one day, when they look into it, they don't see a flaw. They see themselves and they smile.

When the Mirror Becomes a Judge

There are moments in motherhood that break your heart without a sound. One of those moments is watching your daughter stand in front of the mirror; not admiring herself but assessing herself. Measuring. Comparing. Judging.

I've seen Kalpana do this so many times. Quietly, without drama. She'll twist to one side, then the other. Pull her hair back. Let it down. Take a photo, frown, delete it. Then take another. Some days, she'll do it twenty times. Looking for something in her reflection. Maybe for beauty. Maybe for proof that she fits in. Maybe for validation she hasn't yet found in herself.

There are no loud complaints, but her silence says everything. Sometimes she says things in passing; casual, like a joke, but her eyes give her away. *"Ugh, why do I have so much acne?"* *"I look weird from this side."* *"Look at her, she's so pretty. I just look… basic."*

Each word lands like a small crack in a wall I've been trying to build around her; a wall of self-love, confidence and inner strength. And every time I hear her say these things, a voice inside me wants to shout: *"Beta, you are more than your face! You are more than your nose, your jawline, your skin. You are kind, bright, curious, funny. You are art; complex and beautiful and enough."*

But I don't shout. Because I've learned that shouting, even with love, doesn't reach a heart that's under attack, from the inside. So, I breathe. I sit with her. Sometimes I offer a soft truth: *"You're allowed to feel unsure. But your worth is not up for debate."*

Sometimes I say nothing at all; just stay beside her until she's ready to see herself with kinder eyes. She's growing up in a world that is constantly whispering to her: *"You're not enough; unless you look like this."*

And now, the mirror isn't just showing her reflection. It's judging her. It's asking her questions she doesn't know how to answer: Do I belong? Am I pretty enough? Will I be liked, loved, accepted?

I can't stop the world from making her question herself. But I can make sure that when she turns away from that mirror, she finds someone who sees more. Someone who reminds her; gently, consistently; that she is so much more than how she appears. That beauty isn't the goal. Belonging to yourself is.

And every time she chooses to keep going; despite the acne, the doubts, the harsh inner voice; I celebrate a quiet victory. Because learning to love yourself in a world that profits from your insecurity? That's not easy. But she's trying.

And I'll be here, every step of the way, holding the truth until she can carry it on her own: *You are enough; exactly as you are.*

Social Media: The New Mirror

It was a regular afternoon; sunlight spilling through the curtains, the usual hum of chores in the background. Kalpana was lying on the sofa, phone in hand, thumb scrolling through a stream of flawless faces. I walked past and paused beside her, catching a glimpse of her screen.

Perfect skin. Flat stomachs. Glassy eyes. Flowy hair. Selfies edited to symmetry. Lives posed to perfection. She tapped on one photo and stared at it just a little longer. *"Look at her,"* she said quietly, almost to herself. *"She's so confident."*

I sat beside her and gently asked, *"Do you think that's real?"* She didn't answer right away. I could see the conflict on her face; a tug-of-war between knowing and wanting. Finally, she shrugged and said, *"Even if it's fake, I still wish I looked like that."*

And in that moment, my heart cracked open. Because no matter how much we tell our daughters they're beautiful, strong, enough; the digital world whispers a different message in a much louder voice.

Social media has become the new mirror. But unlike the one in our bathrooms, it doesn't just reflect. It distorts. It curates. It convinces. It tells our girls that confidence looks like curves without cellulite, smiles without braces, eyes without dark circles. That success looks like bikini photos at sunset and skin that never breaks out. That beauty equals worth; and everything else is not enough.

And our girls, still figuring out who they are, begin to shrink. Not in body; but in spirit. They start comparing their unfiltered moments to someone else's edited ones. They measure their beauty by likes and their self-worth by DMs. They start to feel like they have to be someone else to be loved. And slowly, the girl who used to dance in the living room without caring who was watching… stops dancing.

That day, I didn't argue with Kalpana or give her a lecture on filters. I didn't say, *"You're beautiful just the way you are,"* because she wasn't ready to hear it. Instead, I said, *"I feel that too sometimes. It's hard not to compare."* Because what she needed wasn't a pep talk. She needed someone to stand with her inside the discomfort. To tell her she wasn't alone in feeling not enough.

Over time, we've started having more of these quiet conversations, about body image, comparison, beauty, worth. I show her unfiltered photos. I tell her about the insecurities I had at her age. I let her see that even grown women feel this pressure. And slowly, I see her lifting her head a little higher.

This world isn't easy for teenage girls. Especially not one where your reflection is judged a hundred times a day with every scroll. But I want Kalpana to know that confidence isn't something you find in a filter. It's something you build, in the quiet spaces between doubt and truth. And that her worth? It was never meant to be measured in followers. It lives in who she is; not how she looks.

My Mistakes

I'll be honest; I've said things I wish I could take back.

Not in anger. Not with cruelty. But in that offhand, careless way we sometimes speak to the ones we love most. In the name of "**guidance**." In the spirit of "**just being helpful.**" I didn't even think twice when I said, *"You looked better before the haircut,"* or *"Wear something that hides your legs; it'll look better in photos."*

To me, they were suggestions. Just motherly advice. Nothing meant to hurt or shame. But to her? They landed differently. Heavier. Sharper. They didn't feel like love. They felt like judgment. Like I was measuring her against some invisible, impossible standard she never agreed to.

One day, after one of those little **"corrections,"** she said quietly, *"Mumma, sometimes you also make me feel not good enough."*

And just like that, I was stopped in my tracks. Shocked. Ashamed. My heart dropped. Not because she was being rude; but because she was being honest. And I had to sit with the hard truth that sometimes, despite all my love, I had been part of the pressure she felt to be different, better, prettier.

That moment changed something in me. I began to look back at how often, as women, we are told; directly or indirectly; that our worth is tied to how we look. How much space we take up. How flawless we appear. And suddenly, I saw how I had been passing down the very messages I had spent my life trying to unlearn.

So now, I try to be more intentional. I try to shift the focus. I speak about her strength, her kindness, her resilience. I tell her that beauty isn't what people see; it's what she carries in her eyes when she's brave enough to be herself.

And this isn't about pretending I've mastered it. I still slip up. I still catch myself making a comment that sounds too much like a critique. But now, I apologize. I explain. I let her know I'm learning, too. Because more than anything, I want her to believe; deep in her bones; that she doesn't have to earn beauty. That she doesn't have to fix or shrink or hide herself to be accepted.

I want her to walk through the world knowing that she is enough, exactly as she is. And if that means I have to relearn everything I thought I knew about being a girl, about being a mother; so be it. Because our daughters are listening. And what we choose to say; and not say; can become the loudest voice inside their heads for years to come.

One Gentle Word at a Time

When Kalpana was younger, confidence looked simple. A gold star on her homework. A high-five after a dance performance. A bright dress she twirled in, certain she looked like a princess. But now, at fifteen, confidence feels more fragile. More layered. No longer something I can just pour into her with compliments.

Because now, she's looking at herself through so many lenses; her friends' opinions, her phone screen, the mirror, her changing body and the unspoken rules the world puts on girls her age. And in the middle of all that noise, I've come to understand that real confidence doesn't just come from praise. It comes from feeling accepted. Completely. Without conditions. Even on the days she's unsure of herself.

So, I started changing how I show up for her, not with louder encouragement, but with softer, more intentional words. I don't say, "You look pretty," as often as I used to. Not because I don't think she's beautiful, but because I want her to know her worth isn't tied to how she looks. Now I say,

"I love how you express yourself."
"You looked so at ease in your own skin today."
"That idea you shared was really thoughtful."

And I let her make her own choices; especially when it comes to her body, her clothes, her style. Even if I don't love the oversized hoodie or the mismatched earrings, I bite my tongue. Because confidence isn't built when someone tells you to fit in; it's built when someone lets you figure yourself out.

I tell her about how awkward I felt as a teenager. How I used to hate my arms or second-guess how I looked in a photo. And how I've learned; slowly, imperfectly; to love those parts too. She listens, sometimes with a smirk, sometimes quietly. But I see it land. I see it ease something inside her. Because when she sees me embracing my own imperfections, she learns it's okay to do the same.

Confidence doesn't bloom in applause. It blooms in silence; when she tries something new and isn't judged. When she wears something bold and no one corrects her. When she's awkward and still met with love. That's what I'm trying to give her. Not just compliments, but permission to be exactly who she is. Without needing to shrink. Without needing to shine all the time. Just enough space and softness to grow into her own skin. One gentle word at a time.

A Real Moment

It was a lazy Sunday; the kind of day that carries no pressure, no plans. The air was still, the light soft and the house unusually quiet. Kalpana had just stepped out of the shower, her hair damp and clinging to her shoulders. She wore one of those oversized, faded T-shirts that she never lets me throw away. No makeup. No styling. No performance.

She wasn't doing anything special. Just sitting cross-legged on the sofa, sipping something warm, staring out the window with that look teenagers sometimes have when they've finally stopped performing for the world and started just being. And in that small, unnoticed moment, I saw something rare. Peace. Not happiness. Not excitement. But the kind of stillness that feels earned; like the storm inside had quieted for a while.

I looked at her and said softly, *"You look so calm. It suits you."* She turned toward me, surprised; not by the compliment, but by the fact that I noticed. Her face softened. A small smile tugged at her lips; not the big, dramatic, Instagram kind. Just… a real smile. Simple. Unpolished. Beautiful.

That moment stayed with me. Not because it was grand or emotional. But because it was true. Unfiltered. Unplanned. Untouched by the world's demands for perfection. And I realised: this is the version of her I want to protect. Not the version trying to fit in. Not the one chasing approval through followers, filters or trends. But the version that feels most like herself. The one she forgets to notice, but I always see.

As a mother, it's easy to get caught in the noise; the schedules, the grades, the attitudes, the eye rolls. But sometimes, in the quiet, we're gifted a glimpse into who they are underneath it all.

And when we see it, really see it, we have a choice.

What I Tell Her (And Myself)

There's so much noise out there. So many images. So many comparisons. So many messages telling our daughters how to look, how to act, how to fit in. It's loud. It's constant. And no matter how grounded we try to keep them, some of it seeps in; through phones, through friendships, through the quiet thoughts that whisper, *"You're not enough."*

I see it in Kalpana sometimes. In the way she stares a little too long into the mirror. In how she hesitates before posting a photo. In the way she asks, *"Do I look okay?"* when she's already beautiful.

And so, I've started telling her things. Little truths. Repeated often, spoken gently. Words that I wish someone had said to me when I was her age; when I was also trying to measure up to standards I didn't understand.

"You are allowed to be different from what you see online."
"Beauty is not a competition; it's a story and yours is still being written."
"Be kind to the girl in the mirror. She's doing her best."

I say them out loud. I say them when she's listening and even when she pretends not to. I leave them in notes. I weave them into everyday conversations. And slowly, I've realized… I'm not just saying them for her.

I'm saying them for me too. Because I still catch myself comparing. Still find traces of that same pressure buried in my own thoughts; when I look in the mirror, when I scroll through social media, when I feel like I'm not doing enough or being enough. And in those moments, I remind myself: if I want her to believe these truths, I have to live them too.

Because in a world full of filters, our girls don't need more perfection; they need authenticity. In a world full of pressure, they don't need more performance; they need peace. And peace begins at home. It begins in the way we speak. In the way we see them. And most importantly, in the way we see ourselves.

If we speak to ourselves with kindness, they learn to do the same. If we model confidence without cruelty, they learn that strength doesn't come from comparison; it comes from compassion.

Chapter 8

Friends, Fights and Frenemies

When Kalpana walked into the house that evening, her face said everything.

No "hi." No "I'm hungry." No eye contact. Just a slow walk to her room and the soft click of the door shutting behind her. I knew something had happened.

Fifteen minutes later, I knocked gently. *"Can I come in?"* No answer. So, I left her tea outside her door, the way I do on days she doesn't want to talk. I didn't ask questions. I didn't press.

An hour later, I found her on the balcony, sitting on the swing with her knees pulled to her chest. Her face was tight, her eyes glassy. *"Fight with a friend?"* I asked quietly.

She nodded, not looking at me. *"With all of them."* Over the next hour, the story came out in pieces.

Group chats. Inside jokes Kalpana wasn't part of. A birthday party she wasn't invited to. Screenshots shared behind her back. And the worst part? One of her closest friends, someone she'd known since two years, hadn't defended her.

"She just stood there," Kalpana said, voice cracking. *"She didn't say anything."* I didn't interrupt. I didn't try to fix it. I just listened. Because I could tell; this wasn't just about the fight. This was about trust, rejection and the fear of not belonging.

Teenage girl friendships are complicated. One day they're sisters. The next, they're strangers. One moment, it's laughter so loud the walls shake. The next, its silent group exits and unread messages.

And yet, these relationships hold so much emotional weight. For girls like Kalpana, friends aren't just friends. They're lifelines. They're mirrors. They're identity.

When something shifts in that circle; even slightly; it feels like an earthquake. I remember Kalpana saying through tears, "I don't even know if I'm overreacting." I looked at her and said, *"No, you're just hurt. And it makes sense. It always hurts when people we care about don't show up for us."*

She leaned her head on my shoulder and whispered, *"Why does it feel so heavy?"* And I told her the truth: *"Because you love deeply. And loving people always carries weight."* Over the next few days, I watched her move through sadness, anger and confusion. Some moments she'd say, *"It's fine, I don't need anyone."* Other times she'd cry into her pillow. Sometimes she acted like nothing happened at all.

That's the thing with teenage girls; they carry their pain in layers. Under sarcasm. Under indifference. Under "I don't care."

But they do care. So much more than they admit. And they need someone to see that pain; even when they're pretending, they're "so over it."

Eventually, Kalpana and a couple of her friends worked things out. Not with a big conversation, but slowly. A shared meme. A short apology. A quiet understanding. But some friendships didn't return. And she learned, in her own way, that not everyone who laughs with you stays with you.

One night, she came to me and said, *"I think I used to ignore stuff just so I wouldn't lose them. But now I feel like I was losing myself."* And I smiled, because she was learning something it takes some people decades to understand. Teen girl friendships will always be messy and magical.

There will be drama. Fights. Group chat exits. Hurt feelings. But there will also be late-night calls, shared secrets and the kind of fierce loyalty that heals. Our job as mothers isn't to control those relationships. It's to be the soft place they land when those friendships feel like too much to hold.

To remind them that one bad friendship doesn't make them unlovable. That being left out doesn't mean they aren't worthy. That they're allowed to outgrow people who make them feel small. Because in the end, as Kalpana's learning. Real friends don't just accept you when you're easy to love. They stay when you're messy. When you're moody. When you're in pieces. Just like we do.

Teenage Friendships Are Intense

When Kalpana was younger, her friendships were simple. They were built on who had the same lunchbox, who liked skipping rope or who brought glitter pens to school. Arguments were short-lived and often resolved by the next recess. Birthday parties, silly songs, pencil box sharing – friendship was joyful, soft and easy to understand.

But something changed when she hit her teenage years. Suddenly, friendship was no longer just about playing together. It was about belonging. There were now group chats where every emoji carried meaning. Inside jokes she wouldn't explain to me. Whispered laughter. Carefully curated photos. And sometimes, complete silence when she walked into a room; followed by that unmistakable ache on her face.

Now, a disagreement wasn't just a disagreement. It was a social shift. A screenshot. A "seen" message with no reply. A meme posted to exclude, not amuse.

As a parent, I was slow to catch on. I'd see her crying over her phone and assume she was being dramatic. *"You'll make new friends,"* I'd say. *"It's not a big deal."* But to her, it was a big deal. Because teenage friendships aren't just about fun anymore. They're emotional lifelines.

For girls like Kalpana, friends become the mirrors through which they see themselves. They are her world outside of us. They are her secret keepers, her mood stabilisers, her validators. And when something cracks in those relationships, it doesn't just hurt; it shakes her sense of identity.

One day, I found her curled up in bed, tears streaking down her cheeks over a single line: *"I don't think we can be friends anymore."* That message hit her harder than any exam result, any scolding, any boundary I'd ever set. Because for her, losing a friend wasn't just losing someone to talk to; it was like losing a part of herself.

What makes it even harder is the intensity of the world she's growing up in. Social media turns every moment into a performance. A missed tag or a group photo can feel like rejection. The lines between private and public blur. Everything is documented. Everything is permanent. Everything is personal.

Teenage friendships are intense because teenage emotions are intense. They love fiercely. They feel deeply. And when a friendship breaks, it's a kind of heartbreak no one warns you about.

But if we can hold space for their pain; without minimizing, without rushing; we give them something more lasting than advice: We give them room to heal.

And maybe, a little more strength to navigate the beautiful, complicated mess of growing up.

"Why Didn't She Invite Me?"

It was a quiet Saturday evening; one of those slow, relaxed hours where the house is soft with weekend stillness. Kalpana was sitting on the sofa, scrolling through her phone when I noticed her posture shift. She wasn't frowning but something in her face fell. Her fingers stopped moving. Her breath caught.

"What happened?" I asked. She turned her screen toward me, showing a WhatsApp status from a classmate. A photo from a birthday dinner; cake, candles, smiles, familiar faces. Friends she saw every day at school. Friends she assumed she was part of. And then she said quietly, almost like she was still processing it herself: *"Everyone was there except me."* I sat down next to her, unsure of what to say. My first instinct was to protect her from the sting, to soften the moment. I offered, *"Maybe it was a small gathering?"*

She didn't look at me. She just stared at the screen and said, *"Nahi, mujhe jaan bujhkar nahi bulaya gaya."* And that was it. No tears. No outburst. Just a kind of stillness that felt heavier than anger. A wall quietly going up. A heart slowly folding inward.

That's the hardest part about these moments. The pain isn't loud. It doesn't shout. It doesn't demand attention. It just sinks, quietly, into the corners of their confidence. And unless we're really paying attention, we might miss the depth of it altogether.

Social exclusion isn't new, but for teenagers today, it's far more visible. They don't just hear about a gathering; they see it, in real-time, in photos, in status updates, in the number of views and likes. The wound isn't just emotional. It's digital. And it reopens every time they look again.

I wanted to say more. I wanted to tell her that she's enough, that friendships are complicated, that this doesn't define her. But I stopped myself. Because this wasn't a moment that needed fixing. This was a moment that needed witnessing.

So, I didn't give advice. I didn't offer false hope. I just placed my hand gently on hers and sat with her. We didn't talk much after that. She got up and went to her room. But later that night, she left her door open. A small sign that said, I'm not okay, but I still want you close.

What I've learned is this: not all wounds bleed openly. Some just sit quietly under the skin. And sometimes, being a good parent means holding space for invisible bruises. Not filling them with words. Just making sure they don't grow in the dark. Because when we honour the silence, the sadness doesn't have to grow into shame.

It can soften. It can breathe. And one day, it can begin to heal.

How I Help Without Hovering

It was a simple ordinary moment; one of those domestic scenes that doesn't ask for attention. Kalpana and I were standing in the bedroom folding laundry. T-shirts, towels, bedsheets. No big conversation. No drama. Just the soft rustle of cotton and the kind of silence that feels companionable.

For a long time, I thought parenting was a one-way street. That I had to teach, shape, guide. That she would grow and I would stay steady. But the truth is, we're both growing at the same time. She's figuring out how to be a teenager, how to name her feelings, how to find her voice. And I'm figuring out how to be her mother through this version of her; this changing, blossoming, beautiful mess of contradictions.

The more I've learned to pause, the more I've seen her doing it too. Fewer storms, fewer slammed doors. More quiet returns. More moments like this one, folding laundry and naming what had changed; not just between us, but within us.

And that's the part no one really talks about when we model emotional growth, they start practicing it too. Not perfectly. Not all at once. But gently. Gradually.

The pause didn't just give me time to calm down. It gave her time to breathe. To realise that she didn't have to defend herself all the time. That our home wasn't a battleground, but a place she could come undone and still be held.

That moment in the room; laundry in hand and hearts wide open; wasn't about clothes. It was about repair. It was about recognition. It was about the quiet reward of slowing down long enough to let understanding rise to the surface.

Because the pause isn't just something I'm practicing. It's something she's learning too. And what we're building together isn't control; it's connection. Not perfection; but presence.

And in that space between her folding and my listening, something sacred happened: We came back to each other; with less noise and more kindness.

When You Become her Enemy

It happened on a regular weekday evening. We were in the kitchen; me making chai, Kalpana scrolling through her phone and ranting about a fight she had with her best friend, Kavya. Her words came fast and heated: "She just said it like that in front of everyone; like I was stupid or something." I could hear the hurt behind her anger, but before I could stop myself, I offered a classic parent reply.

"Maybe Kavya didn't mean it that way?" That's all I said. Just one line. And that's when she exploded. *"You always take their side! Why don't you ever listen to me?"* Her voice was sharp, her eyes furious. It wasn't just frustration; it was betrayal. To her, that one sentence meant I wasn't with her. That I was defending the person who had made her feel small.

In that moment, I felt like a stranger in her story. I had become the opposition; not because I disagreed, but because I didn't fully align myself with her pain. And it hit me: sometimes, she doesn't want a logical parent. She wants a loyal one.

I used to think being a good parent meant helping her see all sides. Offering advice. Making her emotionally "strong" by helping her think clearly. But what she really wanted in those moments? A teammate. Not a therapist.

Now, I've learned to ask something simple. Before I respond to her rants or stories or pain, I pause and gently ask: *"Do you want me to just listen or do you want advice?"* It sounds small, but it changes everything. When she says, *"Just listen,"* I zip my lips, nod and let her speak without interruption. And when she says, *"Okay, what do you think?"*; that's my green light.

It gives her something teenagers are constantly reaching for: a sense of control. But more importantly, it tells her: I'm with you. I see you. I'll sit with your feelings, even if they're messy or one-sided or hard to hear. And what I've found is that when she feels heard first, she becomes more open later. More reflective. Less reactive.

Because the truth is, she doesn't need me to solve everything. She needs to trust that I won't abandon her in the middle of her pain; even if I don't fully agree with her perspective. That's what calms the chaos. That's what keeps me from becoming the enemy. And that's what keeps the door to connection wide open.

Frenemies: The Confusing Ones

There are a few girls Kalpana talks about with an odd mix of frustration and attachment. One day, she'll come home complaining, *"She was so fake today,"* and by the next, they're sharing selfies and eating from the same lunchbox again. It's dizzying to watch; how a friendship can shift from laughter to tension and back again in the span of a single school day. I used to ask, confused, *"Wait, I thought you didn't like her?"* And she'd shrug and say something I've come to hear more often than anything else these days: *"It's complicated."*

At first, I didn't understand. Friendship, to me, had always been simpler - built on trust, loyalty and mutual care. But teenage friendships? They live in a different universe. They're layered with insecurity, group dynamics, popularity, peer pressure and the unspoken fear of being left out. It's not just about liking someone; it's about belonging. And sometimes, even a toxic friendship feels safer than the risk of social isolation.

Kalpana would sometimes tell me stories that made my chest tighten; how a classmate complimented her outfit in the morning and then mimicked her behind her back by lunch. How someone invited her to sit with them at break but excluded her from the group chat later that night.

I wanted to swoop in, fix it, explain how *"real friends don't treat you like that."* But I held back. Because teenage relationships aren't problems to be solved; they're experiences to be felt and figured out.

I started saying things like, *"You don't have to stay close to people who make you feel small. It's okay to take space. Protecting your peace isn't rude; it's necessary."*

She didn't always respond. Sometimes she rolled her eyes. But I could see something shifting. She started noticing patterns. She started naming the way certain people made her feel; drained, anxious, unsure. And that awareness? That was the first sign of her learning boundaries.

The truth is that most teenagers don't yet know how to set healthy boundaries. They're still learning to trust their gut, to recognize red flags, to say **"no"** without guilt. And many times, they're scared to walk away; not just from a person, but from the circle that person is part of.

So instead of trying to force clarity, I've learned to simply stay beside her in the fog. I remind her gently: You can be kind without being close. You can forgive without forgetting. You're allowed to outgrow people, even if you once laughed with them every day.

And slowly, she's starting to believe it. Frenemies are confusing; for her and for me. But they've become unexpected teachers. Not of betrayal; but of discernment. Not of drama; but of self-worth.

And as Kalpana learns to protect her peace, one confusing relationship at a time, I remind myself of this: She's not just figuring out who her friends are. She's figuring out who she is; what she will allow, what she deserves and how she wants to be treated. And that lesson? It's worth all the complicated in-between.

What I Hope She Remembers

There are so many things I want to teach Kalpana. Not just about school or chores or how to be **"a good girl."** But the deeper things. The kind you don't find in textbooks or life skills workshops. The kind that sneaks into your soul during sleepovers and heartbreaks and long walks with people who either make you feel whole; or hollow.

One of those things is **friendship**.

Teenage friendships are beautiful, messy, consuming and sometimes cruel. They can build you up or break you down in a single afternoon. One day it's laughter and inside jokes, the next it's silence and side-eyes in the corridor. And in the middle of all that chaos, I watch her try to navigate; trying to hold on, trying to belong, trying not to lose herself in the process.

I know I can't control it. I can't choose her friends, I can't prevent the betrayals and I can't promise that people won't disappoint her. But I can whisper the truths I hope she holds close; especially on the days when friendship feels more like confusion than comfort.

I hope she remembers that she deserves friendships that feel safe and joyful, not ones built on comparison or quiet competition. That being liked should never come at the cost of being herself.

I hope she remembers that shrinking is not a strategy. She doesn't have to make herself smaller; less funny, less smart, less honest; to fit into someone else's version of **"cool."** The right people will never ask her to dim her light.

I hope she knows that real friends don't keep score. They don't compete. They celebrate. They lift each other up, even when life feels unfair. They clap for each other's wins and stay close during the quiet seasons. And above all, I want her to know: It's okay to outgrow people. Outgrowing someone doesn't mean there was no love. It just means she's becoming more herself; and not everyone will walk with her through that.

Her worth doesn't come from being included in a group chat. Or getting tagged in a story. Or having someone pick her first for a school project. Her worth is not up for debate in someone else's heart. It was whole the day she was born; and it's whole now.

I won't be there for every friendship crisis. I won't see every tear. I won't always know who hurt her or how deeply. But I'll be here. Walking beside her; not to fix everything, but to remind her that she's allowed to walk away from what doesn't feel right. That she's allowed to protect her peace. That she's allowed to choose herself.

Because what I hope she remembers most is this: She is already enough. With or without the circle. With or without the applause. Just as she is.

Chapter 9

When She Pushes You Away

It started slowly. Kalpana stopped sitting at the dining table after dinner. She preferred her room. She stopped watching our Sunday movies. She stopped asking for help with her projects. And most of all, she stopped sharing little things; the way she used to.

Earlier, she used to walk into the kitchen just to tell me what happened in class or how she found a new playlist or what her friend wore that she thought was *"so extra."* But now? Nothing.

I'd ask, *"How was school?"* *"Fine."*

"Anything interesting?" *"No."*

And then she'd disappear into her room, door closed, headphones on. I was there, still cooking, still waiting, still listening... but the stories never came. At first, I thought it was just a phase. Teenagers need space, right? They get quiet. They withdraw. But as days passed, the silence grew louder.

What hurt most wasn't the lack of words. It was the feeling that I was becoming someone she could do without. Someone who was once everything... and now, just background.

Then one night, while making dinner, I asked her to set the table. She did it without saying a word. As she placed the plates, I said casually, *"You've been a little distant lately. Everything okay?"*

She paused. Then looked straight at me and said something I wasn't expecting. *"You love Kunal (her younger brother) more than me."*

I froze. Completely caught off guard. *"What?"* I asked softly.

"You always defend him. You laugh more with him. You're always softer with him. But with me, it's always questions and rules."

I wanted to deny it immediately, to explain, to tell her she was wrong. But I didn't. I paused. Because in that moment, I realised; this wasn't about her brother. It wasn't about who I laughed with or defended. It was about how she was feeling inside. Unseen. Less loved. Compared.

I kept my voice calm and said, *"I'm really sorry you've felt that way. I didn't realise that's how it looked to you."* She didn't say anything. She just continued placing the spoons quietly.

Later that night, I left her a note on her study table. *"I see you, even when you think I don't. I love you in ways I may not always say. You don't have to be okay to be close. I'm here. Always."*

Over the next few days, she was still distant. But her tone softened. Her eyes stayed longer on mine when I spoke. She sat on the sofa while I watched the news, not saying much; but staying near. That's when I understood; when a teenage girl pushes you away, it's rarely because she wants you gone. It's because she's trying to find herself and sometimes, to do that, she needs to step away from the people who know her too well.

But distance doesn't always mean disconnection. We're so quick to take it personally. When they stop talking, we think they don't care. When they close the door, we think they're hiding. When they give us cold responses, we think we've failed.

But really, they're saying:

"I need to feel like I can breathe on my own."
"I need to know I still have control over something."

"I need space to think, not because I don't love you, but because I'm overwhelmed."

And our job, in those moments, is not to chase… but to stay. To be steady. To be available. To be present without pressure. Weeks later, Kalpana came into my room late one night. I was half-asleep. She sat on the edge of the bed and whispered, *"I don't know why I said that about Kunal. I was just feeling really low that day. Everything felt off."*

I didn't say *"I told you so."* I just held her hand and said, *"I know. It's okay."* Because when she pulls away, what she's really testing is this: *"Will you still love me even when I'm hard to reach?"* And my answer, always, is **yes**.

The Withdrawal Phase

It was a regular weekday morning; the kind where everything feels rushed. Kalpana was packing her bag, I was running late for a meeting, the kitchen was a mess. We barely exchanged words. A quick, *"Did you eat?"* from me. A distracted, *"Yeah, yeah,"* from her. The air felt heavy with old arguments neither of us wanted to restart.

But then, as I was gathering my laptop and papers, I smelled it; faint but familiar. Cardamom. Ginger. Chai.

I walked into the kitchen and there she was; standing awkwardly by the stove, stirring two mugs of tea. She didn't look up. She didn't make a big announcement. She just slid one of the mugs toward me on the counter and said, almost shyly, *"I thought you might need it."*

It was a tiny moment. Barely a minute long. No grand speeches. No emotional breakdowns. But to me, it meant everything.

Because for all the eye-rolls and silent treatments and stormy evenings we had survived, this simple act spoke louder than any apology. It said, I still see you. It said, I still care, even if I don't always show it the way you expect.

I didn't ruin the moment by over-praising or getting sentimental. I just picked up the mug, took a sip and smiled at her across the kitchen. She smiled back; small but real.

And in that moment, I realized: connection doesn't always come wrapped in heavy conversations or deep heart-to-hearts. Sometimes, it shows up quietly, in a cup of chai. Sometimes, the bridge between you and your daughter isn't built during the arguments. It's built during the moments when no one is fighting. When no one is trying to win. When someone just makes tea.

Parenting teens can feel like a thousand battles over little things: clothes, homework, phones, attitudes. It can make you forget how much love still lives underneath the noise.

But when I paused long enough to notice; really notice; small moments like these, I realized that Kalpana wasn't drifting away. She was still right here, learning how to stay connected in her own changing way.

And me? I was learning too. That not every repair needs words. Sometimes it just needs warmth, silence and a sip of cardamom chai.

When She Needed Quiet

The hall was bursting with noise. Laughter, loud music, the clatter of crockery and cousins calling across tables. It was a typical family wedding; chaotic, colourful, alive. And there, in the middle of it all, was Kalpana; silent.

She wasn't sulking. She wasn't angry. She just moved through the evening like a shadow; smiling politely when spoken to, but otherwise quiet, almost distant. Family members kept nudging me, whispering, *"Is everything okay with her?"* Someone even joked, *"Teenagers, haan? Always moody."*

I smiled and made excuses. *"Maybe she's tired."* *"Maybe she's not feeling well."* But inside, I was wondering too. Was she upset? Was she withdrawing from us? Later that night, on the ride home, I couldn't hold it in any longer. I turned to her and said, as gently as I could, *"You were very quiet today."*

There was no defensiveness in her reply. Just a shrug and a simple truth: *"I just didn't feel like talking. I wasn't sad. I just… needed quiet."*

That answer hit me harder than any outburst could have. All this time, I had been taught to associate silence with a problem. If someone wasn't talking, they must be upset. Hurt. Angry. But Kalpana's words cracked open something bigger: Sometimes silence is not a wound. It's a rest.

In that moment, I realized; our daughters are carrying more than we can see. Academic pressure, friendship drama, body image struggles, the constant hum of social media noise. Their minds are rarely quiet, even when their mouths are.

Sometimes they don't need a solution. Sometimes they don't even need a hug. Sometimes, they just need space. The freedom to exist without having to perform happiness. The permission to be still, even in rooms full of sound.

Since that night, I've tried to read her differently. When she falls silent at dinner or retreats into her room without explanation, I don't rush in with questions or assumptions. I let the quiet stretch a little longer. I trust that if she needs me, she knows I'm here.

Because the truth is, silence can be just as holy as speech. And respecting her need for it teaches her something important: That she doesn't owe the world her energy. That her presence is enough, even when her words are few. That it's okay to retreat and recharge without guilt.

It's saying, through presence alone: *"You are allowed to be quiet here. You are allowed to simply be."*

Letting Her Have Her Bubble

For the longest time, I thought connection with Kalpana meant constant conversation. I believed if we were under the same roof, we had to talk, share, laugh; something; to prove that we were close. Silence made me anxious. It felt like distance. It felt like something going wrong.

But adolescence rewrote those rules.

I started noticing it little by little; how she would retreat into her room after school, headphones on, door half-closed. How she sometimes answered my questions with a nod or a shrug, rather than words. How asking back-to-back questions like *"Who did you sit with at lunch?"* and *"Did you finish your homework?"* only made her withdraw more.

At first, it scared me. I worried: Is she shutting me out? Is she drifting away? But with time and a lot of mistakes, I learned something powerful: She wasn't rejecting me. She was building her own bubble. And my job wasn't to pop it; it was to respect it.

Now, I try to honour that bubble in small but real ways. I don't push conversation when she clearly needs quiet. I don't insist she sit at the dining table if she needs to eat alone in her room once in a while. I don't demand that she explain every sigh or every tear immediately.

Sometimes, I just sit beside her while she scrolls through her phone, both of us silent, no expectations. Sometimes, I knock softly, leave her a cup of tea at her door and walk away.

These tiny acts don't feel heroic. They feel quiet, almost invisible. But they are profound in what they communicate:

"I trust you to come to me when you're ready."

"You are allowed your own rhythm inside this shared space."

"I'm still here. You don't have to earn my presence with conversation."

What surprised me most is that the space didn't create distance. It created safety. Because when Kalpana felt that she could be silent without disappointing me, she started coming back with her words; her real words, not the ones forced out by pressure or guilt.

There were evenings when she would suddenly plop down beside me on the couch and start talking about her day, her friends, her fears. Not because I pulled the words from her; but because she chose to offer them. That's the difference respect makes.

Letting her have her bubble wasn't letting her go. It was learning how to love her without clutching. It was understanding that connection isn't measured by noise.

It's measured by trust. And sometimes the most loving thing we can do is simply sit outside their bubble, quietly, patiently, faithfully; until they open the door themselves.

The Unexpected Return

There are stretches of time with teenagers that feel like walking through a fog. Days when the house feels quieter; not peaceful, but distant. When you pass each other like strangers in a hallway, offering only mumbled greetings or the rustle of a bag dropped on the floor. During those times, you start to wonder: Is the connection lost? Will she ever come back to me?

Kalpana and I had been moving through one of those fogs. Busy days, distracted evenings, short answers to longer questions. I tried not to panic, not to push. I told myself: Give her space. Let her find her way back in her own time. But part of me ached with the weight of the distance.

Then one evening, something shifted. I was sitting alone on the balcony, a cup of chai cooling in my hand, the city lights blinking in the distance. And out of nowhere, Kalpana came and sat down beside me. No announcement. No invitation. Just her quiet presence next to mine.

She didn't say much at first. We just sat, the silence stretching between us, not heavy, not tense; just there. After a few minutes, she said, *"I had a weird week."*

That's all she offered. No explanation. No details. Just that small thread, offered gently, like a peace offering. Every instinct in me wanted to pull, to ask questions, to open the story. But I remembered all the times I had learned that connection grows best when we give it room to breathe.

So, I simply nodded and said, *"Do you want to talk about it?"*

She shrugged, almost sheepishly. *"Not yet. Just wanted to sit here."*

And that moment; small, quiet, easily missed; meant more than a thousand conversations. Because what mattered wasn't what she said. It was that she came. It was that she chose to sit next to me when she didn't yet have the words to untangle what she was feeling. It was trust. In its purest form.

Parenting teenagers isn't always about the big talks, the heart-to-hearts, the dramatic breakthroughs. Often, it's about showing up again and again; creating a space so steady, so safe, that they know they can return to it, even when they have nothing to say.

And sometimes, that return won't look like a hug or a confession.

Sometimes, it will look exactly like this: Two people. Two chairs. One shared silence. And a bond quietly repairing itself, word by unspoken word.

That night, I realised: It's not the conversations that keep us connected. It's the quiet presence that says: *"You're allowed to come home, even if you don't have the right words yet."*

And that is a connection strong enough to weather any storm.

What I've Stopped Doing

When Kalpana first entered her teenage years, I felt like I was running after a moving train. Everything about her seemed to be speeding away from me; her moods, her conversations, even her hugs. I thought if I just tried harder, asked more questions, stayed closer, I could keep up. I could hold on to the closeness we once had.

But all that chasing only made her pull away further. The more I pushed for answers, the more walls she built. The more I demanded closeness, the more she guarded her space. I was exhausting myself; and her.

Over time and through many painful mistakes, I realized something vital: connection isn't something you can force. It's something that grows in the quiet, in the space where trust is allowed to breathe.

So, here's what I've stopped doing: *I've stopped chasing her for answers.*

When she's upset, I no longer ask a hundred questions, trying to dig out her feelings like some emotional detective. I let her come to me when she's ready. Sometimes it takes an hour. Sometimes a day. But when she speaks, it's real. And it's on her terms.

I've stopped taking her silence as rejection.

There were evenings when she'd sit through dinner barely speaking and I'd feel a pang of hurt; Doesn't she want to talk to me anymore? But now, I understand that her quiet isn't distance; it's reflection. It's her way of processing her world without the pressure of conversation.

I've stopped forcing closeness. I used to hover; hover over her phone calls, hover over her moods, hover over her silences, trying to manufacture intimacy. But closeness born from pressure isn't closeness at all. True connection happens when she feels free, not cornered. So I give her space now. And what I've found is that she does come back; on her own terms, in her own time. And when she does, it's beautiful.

I've stopped panicking over the quiet. There are still stretches where she pulls inward; busy with friends, school, her inner world. I used to see those days as threats to our bond. Now, I see them as natural pauses in the rhythm of our relationship. Just because it's quiet doesn't mean it's broken. Still waters still hold deep currents underneath.

Parenting a teenager has taught me that love sometimes looks like patience. Like waiting without worrying. Like staying close without clinging. And that, I'm learning, is where the real closeness lives.

What I Do Instead

There was a time when I believed that repairing connection with Kalpana meant talking. Talking things out. Talking about feelings. Talking until the air between us felt clean again. But teenagers live in a different emotional world. Their walls aren't always built from anger; sometimes, they're built from exhaustion, confusion or the sheer need for space they don't yet know how to ask for gently.

I learned the hard way that pushing for conversation too soon often made things worse. It made her retreat deeper, made the silence colder. She wasn't refusing to talk because she didn't love me. She was trying to find herself; and sometimes that meant doing it quietly, without me filling in the blanks for her.

So now, when tension lingers in the room, when her door closes a little too firmly or when her eyes avoid mine at dinner, I don't force the words. I practice presence without pressure.

Sometimes that looks like leaving a small cup of chai outside her door. A tiny offering. A silent message that says, *"I see you. I'm thinking of you. No expectations."* No notes. No conditions. Just comfort, quietly waiting whenever she's ready to receive it.

Other times, it's a simple text message: *"I'm here when you want to talk."*

No follow-up. No pressure. Just an open door. And often, it's sitting quietly in the same room; not hovering, not questioning; just being near. Reading a book. Folding clothes. Answering emails. Letting her know that love doesn't always come with demands attached. That I can hold space for her without needing to fill it.

Most importantly, I remind myself, again and again, that distance is not failure. It's not rejection. It's the shape independence takes when it's first being built; awkward, uncomfortable and sometimes a little painful to watch. Kalpana needs to learn who she is without me narrating every step. She needs to stretch into her moods, her silences, her growing pains, without fearing that she's damaging our bond.

And what I'm learning; slowly, imperfectly; is that sometimes the best way to hold on is by letting go a little. What I do instead of demanding connection is trust. Trust that the love we've built will hold, even when words fail. Trust that giving her space doesn't mean losing her. Trust that she knows the way back when she's ready; and that my quiet presence will be the light she can always find.

She's Still Listening

There are days when Kalpana feels like a stranger living under my roof. She moves through the house with her headphones on, her shoulders hunched inwards, her answers short and clipped. I ask about her day and she shrugs. I offer her favourite snack and she says, *"Later."* I call her for dinner and she doesn't come until the third time.

It's easy to believe she's tuning me out. That she doesn't hear me. That she doesn't care. But what I've slowly, painfully learned is this: even when she pulls away, she's still listening. Not always with her words. Not even with her eyes. But with the part of her heart that's watching everything I do.

She's listening to the way I call her name; whether there's patience or irritation lacing my voice. She's noticing whether I respect her space when she says she needs time. She's picking up on the way I handle disappointment, anger, confusion; not just when she's looking, but especially when she's not.

There was a time when I thought connection meant constant talking. If she wasn't chatting with me, telling me about her secrets like she did when she was little, I feared I was losing her. I panicked, thinking every silence was a wall being built between us.

But slowly, I understood that presence matters more than conversation. That consistency matters more than control. And that when she's quiet, she's not testing my love; she's trusting it.

Because when a teenager pulls away, it's not always rebellion. Sometimes, it's survival. It's their way of sorting through the noise inside them without the added pressure of performing for anyone else; including us.

Distance Doesn't Mean the Bond is Gone

One of the hardest parts of parenting a teenage daughter is the slow pulling away. It's not sudden, like slamming a door. It's quiet. It's the way conversations get shorter. The way hugs become fewer. The way she starts sharing more with friends and less with you. It happens so subtly that one day you realize; without warning; that you're no longer her whole world.

At first, it feels personal. It feels like rejection. Like everything you built; the bedtime stories, the whispered secrets, the hand-in-hand walks; has vanished. I spent months wondering what I had done wrong, questioning myself after every small conversation that seemed to go nowhere. Every unanswered "How was your day?" felt like another stone on my heart.

But slowly, with time and a lot of reflection, I came to understand something that changed everything: She wasn't pulling away because she didn't love me anymore. She was pulling away because she was trying to build something she had never built before; herself.

Teenage girls aren't trying to break the bond with their mothers. They're trying to build a bond with themselves. And to do that, they need room. Room to make mistakes. Room to be messy. Room to exist outside of our expectations and hopes and fears.

The bond we have with them isn't broken by that space. It's tested. Stretched. Strengthened. If we can be patient enough to wait, kind enough to not take it personally and quiet enough to listen between the silences; they always come back.

Not as the little girls they once were. But as young women who have made the courageous journey inward; and returned more grown, more self-aware and still deeply connected to the mothers who gave them the freedom to become.

Now, when Kalpana spends an entire day in her room or chooses to go out with her friends instead of sitting with me for tea, I remind myself: This distance isn't the end. It's part of the becoming. And sure enough, she circles back.

Not always with grand gestures. Sometimes with a quiet cup of chai placed beside me. Sometimes with a random *"Goodnight, Mumma,"* after hours of silence. Sometimes with a text message that simply says, *"Missed you today."*

And in those small moments, I see it; the bond we built. Still strong. Still steady. Still sacred. Teenage distance is not a goodbye. It's a brave whisper of *"I'm trying to find myself right now. Please wait for me."* And when we wait; not with judgment, but with faith; what we get back is a bond that's not only intact but even deeper than before.

Chapter 10
Talking Without Triggering

You never listen. That was Kalpana's reply when I tried to explain, gently, why I didn't think it was a good idea for her to go for the school trip. I had barely started listing my concerns; cost, safety, timing; when she cut me off with those four words, said with so much frustration that I just stopped mid-sentence.

I stood there, holding the cup of tea I had made for her and quietly asked, *"What makes you feel that way?"* She turned her head, looked at me like I had completely missed the point and said, *"Because every time I try to say something, you start giving speeches. I don't want a speech. I just want to be heard."*

That stung. But for once, I didn't defend myself. I didn't explain how I was **"just being practical"** or **"just concerned."** I simply nodded and said, "Okay. *I'll listen this time. Tell me."*

That moment stayed with me, long after Kalpana had gone back to her room. Because she was right. So often, my **"concern"** came wrapped in too many words. Advice before empathy. Solutions before space. Warnings before understanding. And she, like most teenagers, didn't want to be corrected all the time; she wanted to be heard. Fully. Without interruption.

I started thinking about how I used to talk to her when she was younger. How I'd get down to her level, soften my tone, ask curious questions and really listen. Back then, she'd open up like a book. But now, she'd shut down before I even reached the second sentence.

I hadn't changed my tone to match her growing need for independence. I was still speaking to the child version of her, not the teenager learning to shape her own thoughts. So, I decided to try differently.

The next time Kalpana looked upset, I didn't ask, *"What's wrong?"*

I said, *"Rough day?"*

She nodded, hesitated, then replied, *"Yeah... kinda."*

I didn't jump in. I didn't say, *"What happened?"* or *"I told you that would happen."* I waited. And slowly, she began to talk. About a teacher who embarrassed her in class. About a classmate who made a joke that stung. About how tired she was of pretending everything was fine.

I didn't give her a life lesson. I didn't even try to fix anything. I just said, *"That sounds really hard."* And she kept going. I've learned that with teenage girls, tone is everything.

It's not just what you say; it's how you say it. The difference between *"Why didn't you tell me?"* and *"I wish you felt safe telling me."* One accuses. The other invites.

Teenagers are sensitive to tone, to energy, to judgment between the lines. Even when you think you're being calm, they can sense when you're preparing a lecture. That's when they shut down. That's when the door closes. But when they feel safe; when they feel like they won't be judged, interrupted or talked over; they begin to open up in ways that surprise you.

One night, after dinner, Kalpana quietly said, *"Maa, I like it when you don't try to fix everything right away."* I smiled. *"I'm trying to get better at that."*

She shrugged, then added, *"It makes it easier to talk to you. I don't have to... filter stuff so much."* That was all I needed to hear. Because that's the goal, isn't it?

So now, when Kalpana is quiet, I don't push. When she's irritated, I don't react with my own. When she shares something hard, I hold it gently instead of rushing to cover it with advice. Because she doesn't need perfect words from me. She just needs presence. And when she feels that she hears me; not just with her ears, but with her heart.

Simple Conversations Feel Like Landmines

There was a time when talking to Kalpana was easy. A question was just a question.

"Where's your water bottle?" "Did you finish your homework?" These moments flowed like small, harmless ripples in our daily routine. But as she entered her teenage years, something changed. Suddenly, even the most innocent conversations felt dangerous. I never knew which words would set off a chain reaction.

If I asked, *"Where were you?"* she heard, *"You don't trust me."*

If I gently reminded, *"Did you study for the test?"* she heard, *"You think I'm irresponsible."*

If I corrected her tone, *"Don't talk like that,"* she heard, *"You don't even try to understand me."*

It was confusing. Exhausting. I started questioning everything I said. Should I ask? Should I stay silent? Should I risk another explosion over something that, to me, felt so small? At first, I thought she was just being rebellious. Overreacting. Acting out. But the more I watched her; the tension in her shoulders, the way she held her breath when I questioned her, the way she snapped first and softened later; the more I realised: she wasn't pushing me away because she didn't care. She was reacting because she cared too much.

Teenagers aren't emotionally distant, even if it sometimes feels that way. They are emotionally sensitive. They are overwhelmed, raw, tender; trying to protect emotions they don't yet fully understand. Everything feels bigger to them. A small reminder sounds like criticism.

A worried question sounds like mistrust. A correction sounds like rejection.

They're not trying to be difficult. They're trying to defend a self that feels fragile and under construction. Understanding this didn't make it easier overnight. I still make mistakes. I still step into conversations thinking they're safe, only to find myself in the middle of an unexpected storm. But it's different now; because I expect it. And more importantly, I no longer take it so personally.

A New Situation: The Group Chat Drama

It was one of those small moments you could easily miss if you weren't paying attention. Kalpana sat curled up at the corner of the sofa, phone clutched in her hand. She kept locking and unlocking the screen, scrolling with a tense thumb, then staring blankly into space. Her whole body was tense; shoulders drawn tight, legs pulled close. A quiet storm was brewing inside her and I could feel it before a single word was spoken.

I asked, gently, *"Everything okay?"* She didn't answer. Not with words. Just a tiny shake of the head and more scrolling, more silence. My first instinct was to dig deeper; to ask, *"What happened? Tell me!"* But something in her posture told me that what she needed right then wasn't pressure. It was patience.

Later that night, as I was chopping vegetables, she slipped quietly into the room. No dramatic entrance. No announcement. Just one short sentence, tossed like a pebble into the silence: *"My friends are planning something without me."*

It hit me harder than I expected. I could see it in her face; the confusion, the hurt, the sudden drop in self-worth that these small social exclusions can bring at that age. Every part of me wanted to jump in, to fix it. I wanted to say,

"Ask them directly!"

"Maybe it's a misunderstanding!"

"Don't worry, real friends don't do that!"

But I stopped myself. Because advice, even well-meaning advice, often feels like dismissal to a hurting heart. So instead, I paused, took a breath and simply said: *"That must feel really lonely."* And that was it; the moment the wall cracked. Kalpana's glassy eyes met mine and for the first time that evening, she let herself lean into me; not physically, but emotionally. *"It does,"* she whispered.

That's when I realised something I keep needing to learn again and again: Validation opens the door. Advice slams it shut too early. She didn't need solutions right then. She didn't need me to make it better or frame it differently. She needed me to sit beside her sadness, not erase it.

And when I did that; when I chose empathy over efficiency; something powerful happened. She didn't get defensive. She didn't pull away. She stayed. It's easy, especially as adults, to want to protect our kids from the sharp little wounds of growing up. We want to shield them from being left out, hurt, misunderstood. But real protection doesn't come from fixing their feelings. It comes from letting them feel; with us right beside them.

And when we honour that sky, cloudy and confusing as it is, we teach them they're strong enough to weather it.

When They Push to See If We'll Stay

Teenagers have a special way of getting under our skin. Sometimes, they say things that feel unfair, even hurtful. Words like, *"You're always on my case,"* *"You don't care what I think,"* or *"You never take my side,"* can sting deeply, especially when all we are trying to do is love and guide them. It's only human to feel the urge to jump in and defend ourselves, to say, *"That's not true!"* and explain all the ways we are trying our best.

But over time, I've realized that defensiveness only creates more distance.

The real magic begins when we pause. Instead of reacting, we lean in with a simple, gentle question: *"What made you feel that way?"* This shift; from correcting to being curious; can completely change the path of a conversation. It transforms conflict into connection, anger into understanding.

I saw this unfold clearly with Kalpana. She was always strong-willed and full of passion, but as she grew into her teen years, her words sometimes became sharp. I remember one evening when she burst into tears after a minor disagreement and shouted, *"You never understand me!"* My heart wanted to jump in and defend myself; to list all the ways I tried to be there for her. But I stopped myself. I took a slow breath and said softly, *"Tell me why you feel that way."*

That moment mattered more than anything else I could have said. Kalpana hesitated at first, unsure if it was safe to open up. But seeing that I wasn't there to argue, she slowly unravelled her feelings; about feeling overwhelmed at school, about pressures from friends, about needing more freedom to make her own choices. Things she might never have shared if I had jumped into defence mode.

Teenagers, like Kalpana, aren't really trying to push us away forever when they lash out. They are testing something much deeper: *"Will you stay, even when I'm hard to love?"*

When we stay calm and curious, we show them that love doesn't vanish when things get hard. We show them that we can handle their messy emotions, their confusing days, their growing pains.

Being there for a teenager is about more than setting rules or giving advice. It's about building trust brick by brick, day after day, even in the hard moments. It's about offering a safe space where they can bring their real, unpolished selves; not just the parts that are easy to love.

Kalpana taught me that when a teen pushes you away with hurtful words, it's often when they need you the most. They are struggling to find their voice, their identity, their place in the world. And they need to know, deep down, that they don't have to be perfect to be loved.

In that small, powerful moment, you may just find that you're not losing them at all. You're meeting them exactly where they need you to be.

Coming Back to *"You Love Him More"*

The next evening, the house was quieter. The storm of emotions from the day before had passed, but a heavy feeling still hung in the air. I found Kalpana sitting alone, pretending to scroll through her phone. I knew that if I wanted to heal what had been hurt, I would have to take the first step.

I sat down beside her, close enough for her to feel me there but not so close that she felt cornered. Gently, I said, *"You said something yesterday… about me loving your brother more."* She didn't look up. She just shrugged, trying to act like it didn't matter anymore. But I could see the truth hidden in her silence; the hurt she didn't have the words to express.

Taking a slow breath, I continued, *"I know sometimes it might feel that way. Especially when I'm caught up in helping him with his schoolwork or handling his problems. But I need you to know something, Kalpana; I love you both. Equally. Deeply. Differently maybe, because you're different people, but never more or less."*

She didn't respond. No nod, no words, no dramatic hug like you see in movies. Just silence. A part of me wanted her to say something, anything, to show she heard me. But I reminded myself; sometimes real healing isn't loud. It's quiet. It's slow.

The next day, I noticed a small shift. Kalpana brought her homework to the dining table and sat near me. She didn't ask for help and I didn't push. We just shared the same space; her working, me nearby. It wasn't a grand gesture, but it spoke volumes. She was rebuilding trust in her own way, at her own pace.

That day taught me an important lesson: Understanding doesn't always come with a "**thank you.**" Teenagers don't always have the words to say they feel better. Sometimes, their way of showing forgiveness or acceptance is simply choosing to stay close. It's sitting nearby without walls up. It's letting you back into their quiet world.

Kalpana's small gesture reminded me that trust is fragile but not impossible to mend. It grows back not with big speeches or promises, but with consistency, patience and presence. When we address their fears; even when they're expressed in anger or sadness; we show them that their feelings matter. We prove that love isn't conditional on good behaviour or cheerful moods. Love stays, even when it's uncomfortable.

As parents, mentors or anyone guiding teens, we need to remember: our job isn't to force healing on our timeline. It's to create an environment where healing feels safe enough to happen naturally. Sometimes, love is shown most clearly not through words, but through quiet actions; being there, again and again.

Choosing Calm Over Control

When you're raising a teenager like Kalpana, there are moments when it feels like you're walking on a tightrope. One wrong word, one wrong tone and the whole conversation can tip into an argument. In the beginning, I often found myself reacting without thinking. If she snapped at me or rolled her eyes, I would demand answers. If she spent hours glued to her phone, I would accuse her of wasting her time. Every conversation felt like a battle I had to win.

But slowly, I started to realize something: it wasn't about winning. It was about connection. If I wanted Kalpana to trust me, to open up to me, I had to stop trying to control the conversation and start focusing on calming it.

One small change made a huge difference: the questions I asked.

Instead of saying, *"Why are you always on your phone?"*; a question that came loaded with judgment; I started asking, *"Is your phone helping you unwind or making you more stressed?"* It was a simple shift, but it changed everything. The first way made her defensive, ready to argue. The second way made her pause and think. It told her that I wasn't there to attack, but to understand.

Similarly, when Kalpana spoke to me in a sharp, frustrated tone, it was tempting to snap back, *"How can you talk to me like that?"* But now, I try to breathe and say, *"You sounded hurt. Do you want to talk about what's really going on?"* Sometimes she still shuts down. Sometimes she opens up. But either way, she knows that the door is open; not slammed shut.

Learning to choose calm over control didn't come easily to me. Every fibre of my being wanted to correct, to discipline, to steer her behaviour back onto what I thought was the **"right path."** But parenting, especially during the teenage years, isn't about constant correction. It's about creating a space where our kids feel safe enough to figure things out for themselves.

Kalpana taught me that when she's acting out, she's not trying to make my life harder. She's trying to be heard. She's trying to figure out who she is. And if I meet her fire with more fire, all I do is burn the bridge between us.

These small shifts in the way I speak to her; softer words, better questions, a calmer tone; have made a huge difference. Our home feels less like a battleground and more like a place where she can breathe. I'm not perfect at it. I still lose my patience sometimes. But every time I remember to choose calm over control, I can feel the trust between us growing a little stronger.

At the end of the day, Kalpana doesn't need me to control her every move. She needs me to believe in her ability to grow, to guide her without crushing her spirit.

And maybe, just maybe, when she feels truly seen and understood, she'll start seeing herself that way too.

A Walk That Changed the Mood

Sometimes, when words inside the house feel too heavy, stepping outside can do wonders. After a few tense days where Kalpana and I barely spoke without sharpness or sighs filling the room, I decided to try something different. That night, after dinner, I casually asked her, *"Want to go for a short walk?"*

She didn't exactly jump at the idea. In true teenage style, she rolled her eyes and asked, *"Why?"* I smiled and kept my tone light. *"Just some fresh air."*

She hesitated, but to my surprise, she grabbed her jacket and followed me outside. We started walking down our quiet street, side by side but in silence. For the first few minutes, neither of us said much. I didn't push. I knew better by now; silence can be uncomfortable, but it can also be sacred.

The cool night air wrapped around us. The sound of our footsteps filled the space where angry words had lived just days before. And then, halfway down the lane, it happened. Kalpana broke the silence, her voice soft and a little shaky. *"I'm tired of school,"* she said. *"It feels like I'm constantly behind."*

I didn't jump in with solutions. I didn't tell her to study harder or manage her time better. I simply nodded and said, *"That's a heavy feeling."* Those five simple words were all it took to open the floodgates. For the next fifteen minutes, she poured out everything; her fears about not keeping up, her frustration with teachers, her worry that she wasn't good enough. It was raw and real and I knew that if I had tried to fix it, the conversation would have ended before it even began.

Instead, I just listened. I let her carry the conversation wherever she needed it to go. I gave her the gift of presence; no judgment, no interruption, no agenda.

That walk didn't fix everything. It didn't erase the stress of school or the emotional struggles she was facing. But it did something even more important: it reminded Kalpana that she wasn't alone. It showed her that she didn't have to carry her worries in silence, that someone would walk alongside her even when the path felt hard.

Sometimes, all it takes to change the mood, to heal a rift, to rebuild a bond, is a quiet walk under the stars and a heart willing to listen.

Talking Without Triggering Isn't About Perfection

No matter how much I try to stay calm, to listen patiently, to respond thoughtfully; the truth is, I still mess up. Parenting a teenager is a messy, imperfect journey. And no amount of reading, preparation or good intentions can make it flawless.

There are times when Kalpana is venting about her day and without thinking, I interrupt her mid-sentence, trying to offer solutions. There are moments when I try to reason with her too quickly, laying out logical explanations when what she really needs is someone to just feel with her. And yes, sometimes my patience wears thin. My voice rises before I even realize it, snapping back just when she's already feeling small and hurt inside.

Each time it happens; I feel a heavy ache in my heart. It's not easy to watch myself fall short of the parent I want to be. It's tempting to either beat myself up or pretend it didn't happen. But I'm learning that perfection isn't the goal. Presence is. Repair is. Humility is.

When I mess up, I try not to leave the broken moment hanging in the air between us. I go back to her. I sit down, look her in the eye and say the words that every young heart needs to hear: *"I'm sorry."* No excuses. No shifting blame. Just honesty and care.

And when I do that; when I own my mistakes; something amazing happens. Kalpana softens. She may not always say much, but I can see it in her body language, in her eyes. She sees that our relationship isn't based on me being perfect or always being right. It's based on something stronger: mutual respect, trust and a willingness to keep trying.

By apologizing and trying again, I am telling her something far more important than anything I could explain in a lecture: *"I'm not here to win this conversation. I'm here to understand you."*

That message matters more than perfect words or perfectly timed responses. It tells her that she is more important than my pride. It teaches her that real relationships are built on forgiveness, not performance.

Every time I apologize, I'm modelling something that Kalpana will carry with her into her own friendships, her future relationships, her own inner voice. I'm showing her that love isn't about never messing up; it's about what you choose to do next. There's incredible power in coming back after a mistake and choosing connection over ego. In those humble, awkward, brave moments, real trust is built.

And in the end, that's what matters most; not perfect conversations, but imperfect love that never stops trying.

Chapter 11

The Silent Tantrum

It crept in slowly, like dusk. Not dramatic. Not loud. Just a quiet, steady pull into something I couldn't name.

Kalpana had been home for over two hours and hadn't said a single word. Her room was locked, her dinner untouched and the only sound I heard was the faint vibration of her phone through the floorboards. No shouting, no slamming, no *"leave me alone"*; only silence. The kind that sits on your chest like a weight you didn't know was there until it started pressing too hard.

It's strange, isn't it? How when children are small, their tantrums come with screams and fists and flailing arms; and yet, it's in their teenage years that the quiet ones hurt more. The ones where they disappear. Where they stop meeting your eyes. Where you feel like a stranger in your own home, pacing the hallway outside their closed door with a cup of tea that grows cold in your hand.

I used to believe tantrums were loud. I used to think that silence meant peace. But I've learned; through nights like this; that sometimes, silence is a scream. Just a quieter one. One that says, *"I'm hurting, but I don't want to be a burden."* Or worse, *"I don't think anyone would understand anyway."*

And that's what frightened me most; that Kalpana might not feel like her pain was welcome here. As her mother, I had spent so many years trying to fix her emotions, shape her behaviour, guide her reactions… that I forgot to simply honour her quiet. To give space to the mess she didn't want to explain. To let her fall apart without fear that I'd rush in with questions or solutions or judgment.

So that night, I didn't knock. Instead, I placed a plate of mango slices outside; her favourite, chilled just the way she liked them; and turned off the hallway light and then I waited.

Not for the door to open. Not for her voice. Just for that stillness to settle, knowing she would emerge when her heart allowed her to. It wasn't until the next morning that I saw the empty plate. Her door was slightly ajar and inside, she was sitting at her desk, scribbling something into her diary. Her face was softer, quieter. Not healed, maybe, but open.

She looked up at me and said, *"Thanks… for not making it a thing."* That one line. It landed somewhere deep inside me. Because for so long, I believed my job was to pull her out of her pain, to make it better. But she didn't want me to rescue her. She wanted me to witness her. To sit outside her emotional walls; not bang on them; but leave gentle reminders that I hadn't left.

And here's what I've now come to understand: when our daughters go silent, they're not shutting us out because they don't love us. They're creating space for themselves, space to breathe through a world that often feels too loud, too demanding, too confusing.

Their silence is not defiance. It's survival. Kalpana's shutdown wasn't a tantrum; it was her nervous system waving a white flag, saying, *"I can't process this right now. Please don't make me."* and as a mother, my power wasn't in dragging her out of it. It was in waiting quietly beside the stillness, showing her that even when she retreats, I remain.

We want so badly to be invited into their inner world. But maybe the invitation comes not through our words, but through our stillness. Through restraint. Through grace. Through knowing when not to speak, not to ask, not to fix. And I will be here. Every time.

Not All Tantrums Are Loud

When we hear the word "tantrum," we often imagine shouting, angry outbursts, slammed doors and loud arguments echoing through the house. It's easy to picture the noise and chaos. But what many people don't realize is that not all teenage tantrums look like that. Sometimes, a teenage girl's biggest breakdown doesn't come with raised voices or dramatic scenes. Sometimes, it looks like complete silence.

There are times when Kalpana doesn't slam a door or yell across the room. Instead, she shuts down completely. She avoids eye contact, she doesn't speak and her silence becomes so thick that it fills the entire house. It feels heavier than shouting ever could. There's a weight in the air, a tension that makes even simple moments; like sitting together at dinner; feel uncomfortable.

The hardest part about these silent tantrums is the helplessness they create. You notice something is wrong, so you reach out. You ask carefully, *"What's wrong?"* But all you get in return is a short, emotionless, *"Nothing."*

You ask again, maybe changing the words, trying to sound gentler, hoping to make it easier for her to open up. Still, the answer comes, *"I don't want to talk."*

And then you're left standing there, unsure of what to do next. You start second-guessing yourself. Should I comfort her, sit close and hope she feels safe enough to talk? Or should I respect her space and leave her alone, even though every part of me wants to fix whatever is hurting her?

You begin to walk on eggshells around her, careful not to push too hard but terrified of pulling away too far. The silence feels endless, stretching through the halls, filling the rooms where laughter and conversation used to live. Dealing with these moments is one of the most challenging parts of raising a teenager. Because when there's shouting, at least there's something to respond to. But silence? Silence leaves you guessing. It tests your patience. It tests your heart.

You want to help, but you learn that sometimes the best help is simply staying nearby; without pressure, without demands. Being there, even if she says nothing. Showing with your quiet presence that you care, that you're available, that your love doesn't depend on her being cheerful or talkative.

Not all tantrums are loud. Some are silent storms raging inside a young heart. And sometimes, the most loving thing you can do is to hold your own emotions steady and wait; wait for her to find the courage and the words to let you in.

When She Stops Responding

Last month, we had been looking forward to something special; redecorating Kalpana's room. It was a plan we had talked about for months, imagining how we would pick out new colours, fresh curtains, pretty lights and little touches that would make her room feel like her own safe space. It was meant to be a fun project, a bonding moment between us.

I went to the store and brought back a bunch of colour shade cards. I showed her ideas I had saved from Pinterest; beautiful rooms with fairy lights, cozy corners and bright, cheerful walls. I suggested we could go shopping together for lights, curtains, maybe even some new artwork. It was something I had thought would light up her face, something we would laugh and dream over together.

But when I sat down with her, Kalpana didn't react the way I had hoped. She sat there, quiet, distracted. She barely glanced at the colour cards. For every idea I mentioned, all I got was a mumbled *"Hmm"* or a quiet *"It's fine,"* without her even looking up.

At first, I brushed it off, thinking maybe she was just tired. Maybe she needed a little time to get into the mood. But as the minutes passed, the heavy feeling between us grew. I finally stopped and asked gently, *"Kalpana, are you sure you're up for this? You don't seem excited."*

She paused for a moment, as if weighing her words. Then, without much emotion, she said, *"Do whatever you want. I don't care."*

Her words sounded harsh, but I knew better. I knew she cared. I could see it in the way her fingers nervously fidgeted with the edge of her sleeves. I could see it in the way she avoided meeting my eyes, as if afraid that if she looked too long, her real feelings would pour out.

Something was happening inside her; something much deeper than wall colours or new curtains. This wasn't about decorating her room at all. It was about feelings so big, so tangled, that they had no clear shape yet. It was overwhelmed, not indifference.

Sometimes, when teenagers shut down like this, it's easy to mistake it for not caring. But more often, it's a heart that's too full; a heart trying so hard to hold itself together that even the smallest thing feels too heavy. Emotions stack up inside them like layers and words seem too fragile to carry the weight. They say *"I don't care"* not because they mean it, but because saying more feels too risky, too vulnerable.

As mothers, as caregivers, what's needed in these moments isn't more questions, more pushing or more problem-solving. What's needed is less pressure. What's needed is a quiet, soft presence; a hand resting lightly on her shoulder, a gentle exit from the conversation, a silent message that says, "It's okay. You don't have to have it all figured out right now."

It's a reminder that she doesn't have to force words when they're not ready. That she's not alone even when she's silent. That whenever she feels ready to talk, there will be someone right there, still loving her, still waiting, without judgment or frustration. Because real connection isn't built through pressure.

A New Situation: The School Competition Fallout

Not every disappointment in a teenager's life comes with an outburst. Sometimes, it shows up in quiet ways that are easy to miss if you're not paying attention.

Kalpana had been excited for weeks about the school dance competition. She had practiced her routine every evening, sometimes losing herself completely in the music, her face lit up with determination. When the day of the audition finally arrived, she left the house with nervous energy, dressed in her best outfit, her hair carefully tied back, hope shining in her eyes.

But that evening, when she came home, everything felt different. She didn't say a word. She headed straight to her room and closed the door behind her. Dinner came and went. Her plate stayed untouched. When I knocked gently on her door and asked, *"Kalpana, are you okay?"* her muffled voice came through the wood: *"I'm just tired."*

I knew better. It wasn't just tiredness. It was disappointment; heavy and sharp, sitting in her chest like a stone. But she wasn't ready to talk about it. She needed space to process it in her own time, in her own way.

The next morning, she got up, dressed for school and went about her routine as if nothing had happened. She didn't mention the competition. She didn't bring up the audition. On the outside, it looked like she had brushed it off and moved on. But I could feel it; the sadness she carried just beneath the surface. I knew that kind of silence. It wasn't peace. It was pain.

And so, instead of pushing her to open up, instead of asking questions she wasn't ready to answer, I decided to simply let her know she wasn't alone. I wrote a small note on a piece of plain paper and slipped it under her door. It said, "I know you're disappointed. I'm proud of you for trying. Always here, when you're ready." No demands. No expectations. Just presence; offered quietly, without pressure.

Kalpana didn't respond to the note. She didn't come out of her room that night with tears or apologies. She didn't say thank you. For a moment, I wondered if the note had even mattered. But two days later, as I was standing in the kitchen, busy with the evening chores, she came up behind me and wrapped her arms around me in a hug. No words were spoken. None were needed. In that silent, unexpected hug, everything was said.

Sometimes, healing doesn't come through big conversations. Sometimes it comes quietly; through small notes, silent hugs and the gentle, patient waiting that says, *"I love you, no matter what."* And sometimes, the greatest comfort we can offer our teenagers is simply this: to stand quietly nearby, ready to catch them when they're ready to fall into our arms.

What I've Learned About Shutdowns

Over time, through all the silent dinners, closed doors and quiet evenings, I've learned something important about teenagers; especially about Kalpana. When they go silent, it's not because they have nothing to say. It's because what they're feeling inside is too big, too complicated or too fragile to put into words right away.

Teenagers often shut down when they feel scared; not of us necessarily but scared of being judged. They wonder, *"What if I say something wrong?"* *"What if they think I'm being dramatic?"* *"What if my feelings aren't taken seriously?"*

That fear can make even the bravest teenager retreat into silence. Sometimes, they stay quiet because they don't want to seem "**too sensitive**." In a world where being emotional is often seen as a weakness, many teenagers, including Kalpana, learn to hide their feelings behind a mask of indifference. They think that if they show how much something hurts, they'll be seen as weak or worse; dismissed.

Other times, the silence comes from fear that their feelings will simply be brushed aside. Maybe they've tried before to open up and felt unheard. Maybe they worry that if they start talking, their emotions will be minimized with a quick, *"It's not a big deal,"* or *"You're overreacting."* So instead of risking more hurt, they choose silence; a heavy, lonely silence that speaks louder than words.

And then, there are the moments when they simply don't know what they're feeling yet. Kalpana has often sat quietly, lost in thought, because the emotions swirling inside her were too tangled to name. Anger mixed with sadness; hope tangled with fear; feelings too complex to sort out on the spot. In those moments, she needed time to understand her own heart before she could share it with anyone else.

Through all of this, I have learned one clear truth: When a teenager shuts down, they don't need solutions. They don't need lectures. They don't need us to rush in and fix everything.

They need safety. They need to know that when they are ready to speak, there will be someone who will listen; truly listen; without judgment, without impatience and without trying to force them to feel better before they're ready. Being that safe place isn't always easy. It requires holding back words we feel desperate to say. It requires being okay with silence, with waiting, with offering love that doesn't demand anything in return. But it's worth it.

It's the foundation that will carry them through their hardest days, knowing they're never truly alone.

How I Create That Safety

One of the most important lessons I've learned through parenting Kalpana is that real emotional safety doesn't come from saying the perfect thing or asking all the right questions. It comes from the small, quiet ways we show up; consistently, patiently and without pressure.

When Kalpana goes silent, when the air feels heavy with things she isn't ready to say, my first instinct used to be to talk; to ask her what was wrong, to offer suggestions, to fill the quiet with words. But I've realized that when emotions are running high, too many questions can feel overwhelming, not comforting.

So now, I stop asking too many questions. I don't push for answers she's not ready to give. I give her space to breathe, to think, to just be. Sometimes, that simply means sitting in the same room without expecting conversation.

Maybe she's scrolling through her phone while I read a book nearby. Maybe we're just sharing the same quiet space without saying a word. It might seem small, but those silent moments speak loudly: *"I'm here. You don't have to perform for me. You're safe."*

There are also times when face-to-face conversations feel too intense for her. When I sense that, instead of pushing her to talk, I send a simple message; a text or a note; something light and gentle that she can read on her own terms.

Other times, I leave small, quiet gestures that don't demand a response. A plate of her favourite snacks outside her door. A handwritten note tucked into her backpack. A soft smile when our eyes meet across the room. No pressure. No expectation. Just a reminder that she is loved, exactly as she is; silent or not.

Because the goal in those moments isn't to "**fix**" her silence. It's not to dig out the words she's not ready to say. It's simply to remind her that she's not alone inside it.

Teenagers need to know that even when they withdraw, even when they can't find the words, they are still deeply seen and deeply loved. They need to know that their presence is enough; that they don't have to explain themselves to be worthy of care.

Creating that safety doesn't require big, dramatic gestures. It requires consistency. It requires patience. It requires being okay with not having all the answers and trusting that, in time, she will come back; not because I forced her, but because she felt safe enough to choose it herself.

And every time she does, it's a quiet reminder that real connection isn't built through control; it's built through unconditional presence.

When I Almost Gave Up

There was a week that felt endless; a week where Kalpana barely spoke to me. She wasn't angry, at least not in the loud, obvious way. She didn't slam doors or shout across the house. But the distance between us grew wider with each passing day and the silence wrapped around everything we did. She would respond to her friends' messages with quick smiles and easy laughter. I would hear her chuckle at memes she saw online and watch her act normal around others; her teachers, her classmates, even the neighbours. But with me? There was a wall.

She was cold. She was quiet. She was distant in a way that felt personal, almost punishing. And no matter how softly I spoke, how gently I asked, the wall stayed firmly in place. Each day, the weight of that silence grew heavier on my heart. I started doubting myself.

One night, after another dinner eaten in near-total silence, I couldn't hold it in anymore. I broke down. Sitting on the edge of her bed, my voice trembling, I finally said the words that had been pressing against my chest: *"It hurts when you push me away."*

For a long moment, she didn't react. She kept her eyes on the floor, her fingers nervously twisting the corner of her blanket. And then; finally; she looked up at me. Her voice was small, but her words carried the weight of days of pain and fear: *"Because I didn't want to disappoint you."*

In that instant, everything shifted. She hadn't been pushing me away out of anger or rebellion. She had been hiding from her own guilt. She hadn't told me she had failed a class test. She had been ashamed; too scared that I would be disappointed, too worried that my love might shrink if she didn't live up to expectations. And so, she had built a wall around herself, thinking it would hurt less if she stayed silent.

That night, I realized something important; something I wish I had understood sooner: Silence isn't always anger. Sometimes, it's guilt. Sometimes, it's a heart too afraid to speak for fear of being judged or rejected. Sometimes, it's a young girl sitting quietly with her own heavy disappointment, believing she has to carry it alone.

As I sat there with Kalpana, I didn't scold her. I didn't rush to lecture about grades or studying harder. I simply held her hand and said, *"You could never disappoint me by being honest. I'm proud of you for telling me."*

Because in that moment, it wasn't about a failed test. It was about building a bridge back to trust; showing her that my love wasn't based on her success, but on her courage to show up, even in failure.

And that bridge; built quietly, patiently, tearfully; was stronger than anything a perfect report card could ever bring.

Silent Doesn't Mean Closed Off

There was a time when Kalpana's silence would send a wave of panic through me. The moment she went quiet, I would start imagining the worst; thinking our connection was broken, that I had lost her trust, that she was slipping away and I didn't know how to reach her. I would rush in with questions, hover around her, trying to pull her back before she drifted too far.

But now, after so many shared struggles and gentle lessons, I know better. These days, when Kalpana goes quiet, I don't panic. I don't rush to fill the silence. I don't assume the worst. Instead, I remind myself of something simple but powerful: Silence doesn't mean the door is closed. It doesn't mean she's shut me out forever. It just means she needs some space; a moment to gather her emotions, to breathe, to sort through whatever she's carrying inside.

Kalpana isn't locking the door. She's simply pulling it halfway shut; a soft signal that says, *"I'm not ready yet, but don't go too far."* And when she feels safe, when she feels loved without condition, when she knows she won't be judged for whatever is weighing on her heart; she'll open that door again. She always does.

That understanding has changed everything between us. Now, when I sense her retreating into her quiet world, I don't knock too loudly. I don't force my way in. I simply stay close enough for her to find me when she's ready. Sometimes that means sitting in the living room reading a book, leaving the door open. Sometimes it means sending a simple message or leaving a favourite snack by her side without a word.

Silent doesn't mean closed off. It simply means she's finding her way back; and my job is to make sure she knows that when she's ready, she'll always have a place to land.

Chapter 12
Empathy Over Ego

Kalpana had forgotten to submit an assignment; again. It used to be so easy to manage Kalpana's world. When she was little, a firm tone and a glance were enough to stop her from arguing. A "no" meant "no," and rules were rules. I was her guide, her comfort, her final word on almost everything and she trusted that.

But now, she pushes back. She questions my reasons. She rolls her eyes at my warnings. She turns quiet at things I thought would make her smile. And sometimes; on the hard days; she speaks to me with a sharpness I never imagined would come from her.

At first, I responded with the only tools I knew: authority, rules, *"because I said so."* I tried to win arguments. I took disrespect personally. I thought if I stayed in control, I wouldn't lose her.

But slowly, I realised something painful and true: I wasn't losing her because I gave her space. I was losing her because I was trying to win.

The turning point came during a small fight over a late-night phone call. I had reminded her for the third time to put her phone away and sleep. She snapped, *"You don't trust me at all. You treat me like a child."*

My first instinct was to defend myself; to say that I do trust her, but that it's my job to be careful. That I knew what was best. That sleep is important and so is discipline and so on. But instead, I paused. I took a deep breath and asked myself, *"Am I speaking from love; or from fear of losing control?"*

And then I said something I hadn't said before: *"You're right. I should've asked, not ordered."* Her face changed. Just a little. But it changed. Because in that moment, I didn't use my role to overpower her. I used empathy to stand beside her.

This shift; from control to compassion; is not easy. It means choosing softness when you feel disrespected. It means listening, even when you're sure you're right. It means letting go of the need to be "obeyed" so you can focus on being understood.

And it's not weakness. It's deep, conscious strength. Because parenting a teenager isn't about being the boss. It's about being the person they feel safest turning to; even after they've made mistakes. Even after they've slammed a door. Even after they've said things they didn't fully mean.

Kalpana once asked me during a calm moment, *"Why do parents always try to win arguments? Like it's a debate."* I smiled and said, *"Maybe because we're scared. Scared that if we don't stand firm, we'll lose you. But what I've learned is that control might keep a house quiet, but only empathy keeps hearts close."*

She didn't respond. But she reached out and held my hand. That was enough. Now, when she challenges me, I try not to challenge her back. When she's frustrated, I don't rush in with solutions. I try to see the girl behind the attitude; the one who still wants to be heard, held and understood.

Because every time I put my ego aside and choose empathy, I see her relax. I see her trust me more. I see her soften in ways that rules never could have created. This isn't about letting her do whatever she wants. It's about showing her that she's not being raised to obey; she's being raised to feel safe in her own voice.

And in choosing compassion over control, I'm not losing authority. I'm gaining something much more precious: A daughter who feels loved, even when she's not easy to love. A daughter who doesn't fear me; but returns to me. A daughter who knows her mother isn't here to rule over her… but to rise with her.

The Urge to Control

As mothers, we carry an invisible expectation; to keep everything under control. We're told, often without words, that our daughters' successes are our successes… and their failures, somehow, are ours too. If they behave well, we are praised. If they slip up, we are judged.

And so, without even realizing it, we slip into patterns of control. We start micromanaging their choices:

"Don't wear that; it's not appropriate."

"Speak nicely; people are watching."

"You're not allowed to do that; what will others think?"

"Why can't you just act properly?"

At first, it feels like we're helping them, protecting them. But in reality, we're reacting out of fear; fear of being seen as a "bad parent," fear of their struggles reflecting poorly on us. It's not really about them. It's about our own anxiety.

When fear drives us, we stop listening with our hearts. We move from empathy to ego, from connection to control. But here's the truth I've learned with Kalpana: Control does not build closeness. It builds walls. Every time I rushed to correct her, every time I tried to shape her behaviour out of fear, I could feel her stepping further away. Not because she didn't love me. But because she needed space to become herself; not a version of her I was trying to mould.

It's tempting to think that if we can just manage everything; their clothes, their tone, their choices; then everything will be fine. But real life doesn't work that way. Our daughters are not reflections of our perfection. They are human beings finding their own way.

Micromanagement teaches them to hide parts of themselves. It teaches them that love comes with conditions: behave, perform, meet expectations. And in doing so, we lose the very connection we long for the most.

With Kalpana, I realized that she didn't need me to control her world. She needed me to trust her. She needed me to believe that even when she made mistakes, even when she stumbled, she would find her way; and that my love would stay steady through it all.

In the end, love grows strongest not when we grip tightly, but when we trust bravely.

A Real Moment: The Text Message Mishap

Some of the hardest parenting moments aren't loud arguments or dramatic fights; they are the quiet, unexpected moments when you see your child's hidden feelings slip out.

One evening, while Kalpana's phone was resting beside her on the couch, a text popped up on her screen. Just a few words; but they hit me like a punch in the gut: *"I'm so done with my mom."*

I froze. For a second, my heart squeezed painfully in my chest. Anger rose quickly; not just anger, but sadness too. The instinct to confront her immediately, to demand an explanation, was strong. I wanted to defend myself to point out how much I had done for her; to correct the image she clearly had in her mind.

But somewhere deep inside, a quieter voice told me to wait. To breathe. To not react out of hurt. So, I said nothing at that moment. I let the evening pass quietly, even though my heart was heavy. And later, at bedtime, when the house was calmer and we were both softer, I gently sat beside her and said, *"I saw something today... and it hurt me."*

Kalpana's face turned red immediately. I could see her body stiffen, her hands fidgeting nervously. She snapped defensively, *"You weren't supposed to see that!"* Her words were sharp, but beneath them, I could feel her shame, her fear of being exposed. I kept my voice steady and said, *"I know. I know I wasn't meant to see it. But can we talk about what made you feel that way?"*

For a moment, there was only silence between us. And then; she broke. Tears filled her eyes as she whispered, *"You make me feel like I'm never enough. Like everything I do is wrong."* Hearing those words hurt more deeply than I could explain. Every part of me wanted to protest; to tell her she was wrong, to list all the ways I loved her, supported her, believed in her. But I stayed quiet.

Because in that moment, it wasn't about defending myself. It was about seeing her pain. And when I put my ego aside, when I chose to listen instead of correct, a door opened; a door that had been closed for far too long.

Kalpana didn't need a perfect mother that night. She didn't need polished explanations or carefully chosen words. She needed to feel heard. She needed to know that even when she was angry, even when she felt misunderstood, I would stay. I would sit in the discomfort with her. I would love her through the messy, broken, imperfect moments too.

That night wasn't easy. It left both of us a little raw, a little fragile. But it also left us closer. Because real connection isn't born in moments of ease. It's born in the moments when we choose to stay; even when it hurts, even when it would be easier to walk away. And sometimes, the greatest act of love is simply listening when it would be easier to defend.

From "Fix Her" to "Feel with Her"

When I first stepped into motherhood, I carried a clear picture of what being a "good parent" was supposed to look like. I believed it meant correcting every mistake the moment it happened. It meant jumping in to teach lessons as soon as something went wrong. It meant making sure Kalpana always remembered who was in charge, who held the authority, who had the final word.

I thought that was how you raised a responsible child, with quick corrections, firm lessons and clear rules. But as Kalpana grew older, as her emotions deepened and her world expanded, I began to realize something: Fixing her was not the same as loving her.

It's easy to believe that fixing every mistake is what love looks like. But often, what our children need isn't fixing at all; it's feeling. It's not correction first; it's connection first.

Now, I try to live differently. I try to pause before reacting; even when everything inside me wants to jump in with advice or discipline. I try to listen before lecturing; even when my mind is racing ahead to solutions. I try to validate her feelings before offering any suggestions; even when those feelings are messy, uncomfortable or inconvenient.

Because when a mistake happens, when emotions run high, the first thing Kalpana needs to know is not what she did wrong. The first thing she needs to know is that she's still loved. That she's still safe. That her emotions; even the ugly ones; are allowed.

I've also learned to ask myself one important question whenever I feel that urge to correct or control rise up: *"Is this about her mistake; or about my pride being hurt?"* And more often than not, if I'm honest, it's my pride. It's my own fear of looking like a "bad parent." It's my discomfort with not being in control. It's my wounded ego, not her genuine need for correction.

Realizing this was humbling. It forced me to look inward instead of always pointing outward. Kalpana's growth is not about protecting my image as a mother. It's about helping her become the person she is meant to be; even if that path is messy, imperfect and full of learning curves.

And the truth is, she doesn't learn best when I rush to correct her. She learns best when she feels understood. She grows when she knows she can make mistakes without losing my love. Parenting isn't about perfection; hers or mine.

It's about standing beside her in the storm, not above her. It's about feeling with her, not fixing her. Because at the end of the day, what matters most isn't that she never stumbles. It's that she knows she will never have to stumble alone.

The Day I Said Sorry First

It started over something silly; something that, on another day, might not have even mattered. Kalpana hadn't answered my call. I had tried ringing her several times, worry building with each unanswered ring. By the time she walked in through the door, safe and smiling at her phone, my fear had boiled over into anger.

I shouted at her without thinking. The words came out sharp and loud, harsher than I intended. And she shouted back; defensive, wounded, matching my anger with her own. Within minutes, the fight was over, but the damage was done. We retreated into silence, each sitting with our pride, our hurt and the words we wished we hadn't said.

Hours passed. The house felt heavy with unspoken feelings. I replayed the argument in my mind, my emotions swinging between guilt and stubbornness. The voice of ego whispered loudly: *"How dare she speak to me like that?"* *"She needs to learn her place."* *"I'm the parent. She should listen."*

But underneath that noise, a quieter voice; the voice of empathy; began to rise. It asked softer, harder questions: *"She's hurting. What's behind that tone?"* *"She's learning how to manage big feelings."* *"She doesn't need more shame. She needs safety."*

And that's when I realized something important. This moment wasn't about winning or proving a point. It was about connection. It was about healing.

Later that night, swallowing my pride and gathering my courage, I walked into her room. She was lying on her bed, scrolling through her phone, the distance between us still thick in the air. I sat down quietly beside her and said, *"I shouldn't have raised my voice. I was worried about you, but I let it come out wrong. I'm sorry."*

Kalpana froze for a second, surprised. She stared at me, wide-eyed, unsure what to say. And then, after a long pause, she whispered, *"Me too."*

It wasn't dramatic. It wasn't loud. But in that small, tender moment, something powerful happened. That's the magic of empathy. It doesn't erase the mistake. It doesn't make the fight disappear. But it makes healing possible.

When we lead with empathy instead of ego, we remind our children; and ourselves; that relationships are not about control. They are about understanding. About choosing to love even when pride screams louder.

What I Try to Remember

Every day, especially during the tougher moments with Kalpana, I remind myself of something important: She's not always trying to be difficult. It's easy to take her sharp tone, her heavy sighs or her cold silence personally. It's easy to believe that her attitude is about defiance or disrespect. But more often than not, it's something deeper. More complicated. More tender. Sometimes, she's just trying to cope. Underneath the surface, her attitude is often a mask; a shield she uses to hide what's really going on. Anxiety about school. Insecurity about friends. Pressure to meet expectations she doesn't know how to talk about.

When Kalpana snaps or withdraws, it's not always because she wants to push me away. Sometimes, she's scared. Sometimes, she feels small. Sometimes, she doesn't have the words to explain the storm happening inside her.

And when I forget that; when I respond with anger or sarcasm; I don't make things better. I make them worse. I confirm her worst fear: that her big feelings are too much for me to handle.

When I take a breath and choose softness over sharpness, Kalpana slowly begins to trust me with her truth. Not always immediately. Not always clearly. But little by little, she learns that she doesn't have to hide. She learns that she can bring her messy, complicated emotions to me; and still be loved. That's the real power of empathy.

Empathy doesn't mean letting go of boundaries. It doesn't mean saying, *"Anything you do is okay."* It doesn't mean ignoring disrespect or allowing hurtful behaviour. Boundaries are still important. They teach responsibility. They teach respect for others and for oneself. But empathy changes the way I hold those boundaries.

Every day, I remind myself: Kalpana's journey is not about making me look good. It's about helping her become strong, resilient and whole, even if that means walking with her through the messy parts too. And that's what love looks like: Not control. Not perfection. But connection; the kind that stays steady, even when the waters get rough.

What I Tell Her (And Myself)

There are certain things I try to say to Kalpana often; not just when things are going smoothly, but especially when things are hard. Words that I hope will stay with her long after the arguments, the silences and even the teenage years pass.

I tell her: *"You're allowed to mess up. I still love you."* Because she needs to know that love isn't something she has to earn with good grades, good behaviour or perfect decisions. She needs to know that my love isn't fragile, that it won't shatter just because she stumbles. She needs to know that even when she gets it wrong; especially when she gets it wrong; I will be right here.

I also tell her: *"I want to understand what you're feeling; even if I don't always agree."* Because understanding doesn't require agreement. I don't have to see the world exactly the way she does to honour her feelings. Listening isn't about approving. It's about respecting her emotional world, trusting that her feelings are real and important; even if they're different from mine.

And most of all, I remind her; and myself: *"We're both learning how to do this."* There's no manual for parenting. No step-by-step guide for raising a strong, sensitive, independent daughter. And there's no manual for being a teenager either; for growing into yourself in a messy, confusing, beautiful world. We're both figuring it out as we go, making mistakes, apologizing, trying again.

Because parenting isn't a power game. It's not about winning arguments or demanding respect out of fear. It's not about proving that I'm right and she's wrong. Parenting is a relationship. A living, breathing bond that requires humility, patience and an open heart. A connection that gets stronger not by control, but by compassion.

Chapter 13

Safe Spaces & Soft Landings

Kalpana didn't say a word when she came home from her biology test. Not even a *"hi."* She went straight to the sink, washed her hands and sat down at the table, scrolling on her phone like her mind was somewhere far away.

I placed her tea next to her and asked, *"How did it go?"* She shrugged. *"It was okay."*

But I knew it wasn't. I could see the quiet in her shoulders. Her fingers trembled slightly around the cup and she wasn't really scrolling; just tapping aimlessly. Still, I said nothing.

Later that evening, I walked past her room and found her just sitting on the floor with her back against the wall, staring blankly at a stack of flashcards. I stood there for a moment, debating whether to enter or give her space.

When I finally walked in and sat beside her, she said without turning her head, *"I blanked out in the middle of the test. My brain just... stopped. I knew the answer, but it was like everything disappeared."*

She looked down at her hands. *"It was like I failed before I even finished."* That's when I understood; she didn't need motivation. She didn't need a pep talk. She didn't even need reassurance.

She just needed room to say that out loud without feeling small. So, I said quietly, *"That sounds really scary, Kalpana and I'm sorry it happened."*

No *"you'll do better next time."*

No *"you should've revised more."*

Just space. A moment where she could release what she was holding without fearing my reaction. After a pause, she asked, *"Have you ever felt like that? Like... you're just frozen in the middle of something?"*

I nodded. *"Yes. During my first office presentation, I forgot my own name for a full minute. I stood there holding my notepad, heart pounding, while the projector warmed up and my brain went completely blank."*

She laughed. Just a little. But it was real. Safe spaces aren't built through rules. They're built through emotional permission slips; tiny reminders that it's okay to not be okay here. And those safe landings don't always look like deep talks or teary hugs.

Sometimes, they look like:

Letting her cancel plans with relatives without guilt when she says, *"I'm just not feeling social today."*

Sitting beside her in silence after a bad day, both of us on our phones, not talking, just knowing the other is there.

Saying, *"I hear you,"* even when she's ranting about something that sounds silly from the outside.

Because what sounds silly to us might be the heaviest thing on her shoulders right now. A few days ago, Kalpana got upset over something in school; some rumour, something said behind her back. She didn't tell me right away. I found out only because her classmate's mom mentioned the drama in passing.

When I gently asked her about it, she stiffened. *"I don't want to talk about it,"* she said. My old instinct would've kicked in. Why not? Why do you shut me out? Why do I have to hear things from other people?

But instead, I paused. Took a breath. And said, *"Okay. You don't have to talk. I just wanted you to know that I'm not going to judge you for whatever happened."* She didn't respond. But she didn't walk away either.

An hour later, she walked into the kitchen while I was cleaning up and quietly said, "They twisted my words. I didn't even say what they're saying I said." And just like that, the wall crumbled, on its own time.

We spend so much of parenting trying to teach our children how to behave in the world. But just as important is teaching them how to return home to themselves. And that lesson starts with how they feel in our presence.

Not managed. Not corrected. Not improved. Just held. A soft landing isn't a luxury. It's a necessity. It's the feeling of knowing you can break… and still be met with open arms. It's hearing, *"You can tell me anything,"* and actually believing it.

I don't always get it right. Some days I still slip into my fix-it mode. But more and more, I am learning that Kalpana doesn't need me to solve her. She needs me to receive her; as she is. Because the world will ask her to perform, to prove, to perfect.

But at home, I want her to feel something else entirely:

You don't need to be stronger than your sadness.
You don't need to explain your silence.
You don't need to earn your comfort.

This is your soft place to land. And I'll hold it for you, **always**.

What Is a "Safe Space"

When we talk about creating a safe space for our children; especially our daughters; it's important to understand what that really means. A safe space isn't about being perfect. It's not about being the parent who always says the right thing, who never gets frustrated or who magically avoids every conflict.

It's not about saying "yes" to everything, either. It's not about abandoning rules, boundaries or guidance just to keep the peace. It's also not about ignoring real issues, pretending that problems don't exist just to avoid uncomfortable conversations.

Creating a safe space is something deeper. Something quieter. Something much more powerful. A safe space is about being a soft place to land when the world outside feels too harsh, too demanding, too overwhelming. For a teenage girl like Kalpana, it means a few very specific and very sacred things.

It means knowing she won't be judged when she messes up. Knowing that when she brings her mistakes, her regrets, her bad decisions into the light, she won't be met with shame or cold disappointment. Instead, she will be met with understanding, maybe some gentle guidance, maybe some hard conversations, but never rejection.

It means trusting that she can share something scary without fear of being shouted at. That even when she confesses something that rattles me, surprises me, even worries me, I won't respond with anger that shuts her down. Instead, I'll respond with the steady, patient love that invites her to keep talking instead of closing up.

It means feeling that her emotions; big or small, loud or quiet; are welcome. Whether it's tears over a friendship, anger about a bad grade or fear she can't yet put into words; all of it has a place here. She doesn't have to shrink her feelings to fit into a neat box to be accepted.

And most of all, it means believing she is loved even when she's not at her best. Even when she's irritable. Even when she says things she doesn't fully mean. Even when she's messy, loud, silent, emotional, distant; all the complicated, beautiful things teenagers are. Love stays.

That's what a real safe space looks like. Not perfection. Not blind approval. Not ignoring real problems. But creating an environment where honesty is met with patience. Where mistakes are met with growth. Where love is not a prize for good behaviour, but a promise that never wavers.

A Real Moment: The *"I Failed"* Confession

Some of the most important moments in parenting don't happen during celebrations or big successes. They happen in quiet, vulnerable moments; moments when our children come to us carrying more fear than pride.

One evening, Kalpana approached me with a look I recognized instantly, a mixture of fear, shame and hope. She stood there, hesitating, as if deciding whether to speak or retreat.

Finally, in a voice so small I almost missed it, she said, *"I think I'm going to fail in Maths."* She wasn't dramatic. She wasn't angry. She was trembling; physically trembling; waiting for me to react, bracing herself for disappointment, for anger, for the kind of reaction that would make her feel even smaller than she already did.

For a split second, my instincts battled inside me. The old voices of panic wanted to rise; the ones that said, *"How could this happen?"* or *"You should have studied harder!"* But I caught myself. I took a deep breath and made a different choice.

I looked at her, saw the fear in her eyes and said softly, *"Okay. Let's figure out what you need. Do you want help or do you just need a hug right now?"* There was a pause; a long, fragile pause; and then she whispered, *"Just a hug. I feel like such a loser."*

In that moment, the last thing she needed was a lecture. The last thing she needed was panic or pressure. What she needed was love. Reassurance. A place where failure didn't cost her belonging. So, I hugged her. Tight. Without words, without advice, without conditions. Just arms around her, holding her shame and fear without trying to fix them.

Later that week, something beautiful happened. Without any pressure from me, without lectures or scolding, Kalpana came to me on her own and asked, *"Can you help me with Maths? I don't want to feel stuck anymore."*

Because that's what emotional safety does. It turns fear into trust. It turns silence into conversations. It transforms shame into courage. When children know they won't be attacked for their failures, they don't have to hide. They don't have to pretend. They can reach out, ask for help and believe that their worth isn't measured by their report card.

Creating Safe Spaces Without *"Soft Parenting"*

When we talk about creating emotional safety for our daughters, it's easy for others to misunderstand what that really means. Some people hear "safe space" and assume it means no rules, no boundaries, no consequences; that we are letting them walk all over us, that we are giving up authority just to stay on their good side.

But real emotional safety is nothing like that. It doesn't mean parenting without limits. It doesn't mean saying "yes" to everything. And it definitely doesn't mean abandoning our role as guides and protectors.

Emotional safety is about how we set limits; not whether we set them. It's about setting clear, strong boundaries; but doing it with love instead of fear. With connection instead of control. It's about saying: *"You're allowed to be angry, but you're not allowed to scream at me."* Acknowledging the emotion; validating that anger is a normal, human feeling; but also holding firm that respect still matters.

It's about saying: *"I won't read your diary, but if you want to talk, I'm here." Giving* her the privacy she needs to grow and explore her inner world, while also making it clear that she doesn't have to face her struggles alone.

It's about saying: *"You don't have to tell me everything. But if something feels too heavy, you don't have to carry it by yourself."* Respecting her boundaries while reminding her that support is always within reach.

Creating a safe space doesn't mean removing all discomfort. It doesn't mean that everything feels easy all the time. It means building an environment where hard conversations can happen without fear. Where mistakes are met with guidance, not punishment. Where big feelings are welcomed, but harmful behaviour is gently corrected.

It's not "soft parenting" in the way critics might use the term. It's strong, conscious parenting; choosing patience when anger would be easier, choosing presence when punishment would be quicker. It's teaching our daughters that while their feelings are always valid, their actions still have consequences. That love is unconditional, but respect and trust are things we work to protect and rebuild together.

Setting boundaries with love isn't about giving up our authority. It's about redefining what authority looks like; not as control or dominance, but as leadership rooted in empathy, wisdom and care. In the end, the goal is not to raise a daughter who fears us. It's to raise a daughter who trusts us enough to bring us her truth; messy, complicated and real; knowing that she will be met not with shame, but with strength and love.

What I Changed at Home

Over time, through many hard conversations and even harder silences, I realized that if I wanted real connection with Kalpana, something had to change. And that "**something**" wasn't just her behaviour. It was mine.

I stopped waiting for her to adjust first. I stopped believing that fixing her emotions or controlling her reactions would bring us closer. Instead, I began changing what I could control; myself, my habits, my approach.

I stopped reacting immediately. I started pausing. When Kalpana said something that hurt or frustrated me, I no longer snapped back without thinking. Instead, I tried to take a breath. Even a few seconds of silence made a difference; a small space where empathy could enter before anger could take over. Sometimes I still stumbled, but the intention to pause changed the energy between us.

I created a "**no judgment zone**." A space where she could cry, vent, rant or even say irrational things without being corrected immediately. When Kalpana poured out her worries, I resisted the urge to jump in with advice or solutions. I learned to sit with her pain without trying to fix it. To listen not with the goal of responding, but with the goal of understanding.

I let her have emotional privacy without seeing it as rejection. There were days when Kalpana needed space; when she retreated to her room or gave short answers. I learned not to take it personally. Her needing time alone wasn't a sign that she didn't trust me. It was a sign that she was learning to process her feelings in her own way, at her own pace.

I stopped commenting on her mood unless she wanted to share. If she looked upset, I didn't say, *"What's wrong with you?"* or *"You seem grumpy."* Instead, I would offer simple invitations: *"Rough day? I'm here if you want to talk."* And if she didn't respond, I let it be. I gave her the space to come to me when she was ready, without pressure.

Slowly, I saw Kalpana soften. I saw her share more, trust more, lean in more. And I realized: When we create safety at home; not by lowering standards, but by raising empathy; everything changes. Because teenagers don't need perfect parents. They need parents who are willing to grow alongside them.

One Small Gesture That Changed Things

As Kalpana grew older, I realized that connection doesn't only come from big talks or grand gestures. Sometimes, it's built through small habits; quiet rituals that offer comfort, strength and a sense of belonging.

One of the habits I gently encouraged at home was taking a few moments each day to pray. Not as a forced rule. Not as another chore on her list. But as a small, quiet anchor; something she could return to when the world felt overwhelming.

At first, she wasn't very interested. Teenagers have their own battles, their own doubts. When I suggested it, she gave a half-hearted nod. Sometimes she would sit down for a few seconds, mumble a few words and rush off. Other times, she simply stayed silent, fidgeting, unsure what to say.

But I didn't push. I didn't scold. I didn't make it about obedience. Instead, I made it about invitation, and example. I started lighting a small *'dia'* each evening. I would sit quietly in one corner, close my eyes and whisper my prayers: sometimes only for a minute or two. No pressure. No expectation. Just presence.

And slowly, something changed. Some days, Kalpana would drift into the room while I was sitting there. She wouldn't say anything, but she would sit down nearby. Not always praying. Sometimes just being. Sometimes, just breathing.

Other days, she would ask small questions. *"Do you think God listens when we're angry?" "Can I pray even if I don't know the right words?"*

I always answered the same way: *"There's no wrong way to reach out to God. He listens to hearts, not just words."* This small habit; this gentle space for prayer; became something sacred between us. Not something heavy. Not something forced. But something safe. A place where she could bring her worries, her fears, her gratitude, without judgment.

Over time, Kalpana began making it her own. Lighting her own *'dia'* when she needed courage for a hard day. Whispering small prayers under her breath before exams. Turning to faith not out of habit alone, but out of trust, because it had been offered to her freely.

Teaching her to pray wasn't about control. It wasn't about making her follow rules. It was about giving her another anchor for life; something she could carry in her heart when I wasn't there to guide her.

Because in the end, the habits that last are the ones rooted in love, not fear. And sometimes, the greatest gift we can give our children is not a thousand answers; but the quiet reminder that they are never truly alone.

The World Outside Can Be Harsh

Every day, I remind myself that the world Kalpana is growing up in isn't easy. It's a world that demands a lot from her, often more than she can explain.

School brings its own kind of pressure. Assignments, exams, deadlines; a constant ticking clock telling her she has to perform, achieve, succeed. There's little room for mistakes, little space for simply being young and learning at her own pace.

Then there's social media; a whole different kind of pressure. A world where every photo, every post, every comment is measured and compared. Where she sees endless images of perfection and can't help but wonder if she's falling behind. If she's good enough. Pretty enough. Smart enough. Liked enough.

Friendships, too, are no longer simple. They're unpredictable, shifting with moods, misunderstandings and insecurities. One day they are strong; the next day, a small argument can turn into a cold silence. Kalpana is constantly navigating emotional landscapes she doesn't always understand.

And if that wasn't enough, her own body feels like it's changing without her permission. Growing, shifting, surprising her; sometimes making her feel powerful and sometimes making her feel like a stranger to herself.

The world outside her door is already a battlefield. A place where she's expected to fight, compete, compare and hold herself together even when she feels like crumbling inside.

She doesn't need home to be another battle zone. She doesn't need home to be another place where she has to perform, defend or explain herself. She needs home to be her recharge station. Her safe place. The place where the Armor can come off, where the expectations can fall away, where she can breathe; really breathe; without fear of judgment.

Home should be where she can fall apart if she needs to. Where she can cry without being told she's overreacting. Where she can rebuild at her own pace, in her own way. Where she can be seen, not for her achievements, not for her image, but for her heart. Because when the world outside is harsh, what our daughters need most is not more pressure at home; but a place where they are understood, supported and believed in, no matter what.

What I Want Her to Feel at Home

When I think about everything, I'm trying to give Kalpana, it isn't just advice or discipline or structure. More than anything, what I want her to feel when she walks through our door is relief. A deep, bone-deep sense that she can finally set down all the burdens she's been carrying.

No matter how messy her day was, no matter how much she struggled, no matter what mistakes she made; she doesn't have to brace herself for criticism the moment she comes home. She can let her guard down. She can be her real, raw, complicated self without fear.

I want her to feel, *"I don't have to pretend here."* Outside, she might have to wear different faces; the good student, the loyal friend, the cheerful daughter. But at home, she doesn't have to perform. She doesn't have to smile when she feels sad or act strong when she feels small. Home is the place where she can just be; whatever that looks like on any given day.

I want her to know, deep in her bones, *"Even if I disappoint her, my mom still loves me."* Because there will be disappointments. There will be times she makes choices I wouldn't have made. There will be moments she falls short; of her own expectations, of mine, of the world's. And in those moments, she needs to know that my love isn't on trial. It doesn't rise and fall with her performance. It is steady. It stays.

Most of all, I want her to feel, *"Here, I can breathe."* When everything else feels overwhelming; school, friendships, expectations, even her own doubts; I want home to be the place where she exhales. Where she doesn't have to explain or defend her feelings. Where silence is okay. Where laughter is easy. Where she can find her balance again.

Because before she can be strong out there; in a world that will test her, stretch her, sometimes bruise her; she needs a soft place in here. A place that restores her, believes in her and reminds her of who she truly is.

Strength isn't built by throwing someone into the storm without shelter. It's built by giving them a safe harbour they can always return to. A place where they are loved not for what they do, but simply for who they are.

Chapter 14

Rewriting the Story Together

There was a time I thought parenting meant writing my daughter's story for her; carefully choosing her chapters, editing her mistakes, deleting the lines I thought would hurt her. I believed that if I was careful enough, I could shield her from the messy parts. The heartbreaks. The rejections. The inner battles.

But now, I see it differently. Now, parenting feels more like sitting beside her while she holds the pen.

She writes. I read. Sometimes I guide her gently. Sometimes I just listen.

And slowly, we're learning how to rewrite parts of her story; not to erase the pain, but to understand it better. The shift began after a moment I didn't expect.

Kalpana had just come out of a phase of quiet withdrawal. For weeks, she'd been distant; doing her chores, attending school, smiling at the right times; but clearly carrying something heavy beneath it all. I had given her space, checked in softly, but she hadn't opened up.

Then one Sunday afternoon, while we were folding laundry together; something we usually did in silence; she suddenly said, *"Do you ever think you're too emotional? Like... you feel too much and people get tired of you?"*

I looked at her. The basket of clothes between us. A mix of her T-shirts and my dupattas. *"I used to,"* I replied. *"Especially when I was younger. I thought people would only stay if I kept it all together."* She nodded. *"Me too."*

That was it. No dramatic reveal. No sudden tears. Just a moment of recognition. Of rewriting the story, she had been telling herself; that feeling deeply was a flaw. That being sensitive made her weak.

We started having more conversations like that. Short, quiet reflections. Moments where I didn't play the "wise parent," but showed her I was still figuring things out too.

Once, she showed me an old photo of herself from two years ago; grinning awkwardly, braces and all, holding a school trophy. *"I don't like her,"* she said. *"I was so fake back then. I just wanted everyone to like me."*

I paused. Then said, *"Maybe you weren't fake. Maybe you were just trying to be safe. That's not weakness, Kalpana. That's survival."* She stared at the picture for a moment longer, then whispered, *"I never thought of it that way."*

That's the magic of rewriting stories; not to cover pain with positivity, but to see yourself with more compassion than before. She's learning to tell her own truths now.

When she messes up, she says, *"I didn't handle that well,"* instead of blaming others. When she's proud of herself, she says it out loud, even if her voice shakes. When she's hurting, she still withdraws sometimes; but she comes back quicker and stronger.

And I've started asking her new kinds of questions; not about her marks or her friends or how much she ate; but things like:

"What do you think you needed today that you didn't get?"

"If you could talk to the version of you from last year, what would you say?"

"Where do you feel most like yourself these days?"

Not because I expect wise answers. But because those questions open the door to self-awareness, not just compliance.

Parenting a teenager is not about having all the answers. It's about becoming the mirror that doesn't distort who they are. That reflects both their light and their shadows with softness.

Kalpana once said, *"Sometimes I wish I could erase parts of me. Like the version who got too attached. Or said too much. Or cried in front of people."* I told her, *"You don't need to erase those parts. You just need to hold them gently. They're not mistakes. They're your becoming."*

And that's what we're doing now. We're sitting with her story together; page by page, memory by memory. Some chapters are messy. Some make her cringe. Some still hurt to look at. But she's learning to read them all without shame.

To see the girl she was with love.

To meet the girl she is with honesty.
And to shape the girl she's becoming with courage.

Not just because of me. But with me.

Why Reflection Matters

Our daughters are growing up in a world that pulls at them from every direction. They are juggling mood swings, emotional highs and lows, moments of self-doubt and bursts of confidence that sometimes last just a few hours. They're navigating the confusion of identity; trying to figure out who they are, who they're supposed to be and who they want to be. They're caught in the middle of social pressure; from classmates, social media and even from themselves.

And in the middle of all that noise, there's very little space for reflection. Teenage life moves fast. They often go from one situation to the next; one emotional moment to another; without stopping to look back and ask, *"What just happened inside me?"*

As mothers, we can't protect our daughters from every hard moment. We can't prevent every overreaction or mistake. And we definitely can't write their story for them as much as we may want to. But what we can do is help them learn to pause. To reflect. To look inward, not with shame but with compassion.

We can create a home where it's normal to talk about feelings, not just after they explode, but quietly, when the dust has settled. We can ask gentle questions that invite reflection without demanding a response. We can share our own process; admit when we've overreacted, talk through what we learned, model what it looks like to pause and make meaning out of messy moments.

Because when reflection is modelled, it becomes possible. And when it becomes possible, it becomes a habit. And slowly, our girls learn to see their own story not as something to hide from or regret; but as something they can keep shaping, keep understanding and keep growing from.

When the Street Doesn't Feel Safe

It was a normal afternoon; nothing unusual. Kalpana had gone out with a few friends for a quick snack after school. It was the kind of simple freedom we'd slowly been giving her; something she had earned through trust and responsibility.

But when she came back, she didn't say much. She barely touched her food, avoided eye contact and seemed lost in thought. I didn't push. I waited.

Later that evening, as I sat folding clothes in our room, she quietly entered and sat beside me. After a pause, she said, *"Some boys on a bike kept following us today. They were laughing and saying things. It felt... disgusting."*

My hands froze mid-fold. There was a tightness in her voice, part anger, part shame and a lot of confusion. She wasn't crying. But she was clearly shaken. And more than anything, she was wondering how I would respond.

Would I get angry? Would I ask why she didn't dress differently? Would I tell her to stop going out with friends? Would I scold her for being on that street in the first place?

I didn't do any of those things. Instead, I took a deep breath and said, *"I'm so sorry that happened. That wasn't your fault. That should never happen to anyone."* Her shoulders relaxed; just slightly. It was clear she'd been bracing for blame.

We talked for a long time that night. Not just about the incident, but about how common this kind of harassment is for girls. How it makes them shrink, second-guess and sometimes even feel guilty, for simply existing in public spaces. And how wrong that is.

We talked about safety; yes. About what to do in those moments, who to call, how to stay alert. But we also talked about power. That her voice, her discomfort, her fear; they were real, valid and worthy of attention. That she didn't need to bury the experience or act like it didn't affect her.

"What they did says something about them," I told her. *"Not about you."*

That night, we didn't solve everything. We didn't have perfect answers. But we started something important; a conversation about dignity, boundaries and courage. Kalpana learned that evening that she could tell me even the most difficult truths. That I wouldn't respond with shame, but with strength. That I wouldn't protect her by limiting her, but by standing with her.

And I learned something too: That part of raising a daughter is preparing her for a world that might not always treat her with kindness; but reminding her that she still gets to own her space, her story and her worth. Because one day, when she speaks up; not just to me, but to the world; I want her to remember: Her voice matters. And she never has to stay silent to stay safe.

Helping Her Reflect, Not Regret

Teenagers often carry guilt far more heavily than they show. It doesn't always appear in obvious ways like tears or apologies. Sometimes, it hides behind anger, silence, eye-rolls or defensiveness. They don't always have the emotional vocabulary to name what they are feeling, so guilt festers quietly inside them, building walls instead of bridges.

Kalpana, like many teenagers, would often react sharply or shut down completely after a mistake, not because she didn't care, but because she didn't know how to face the discomfort her actions created. Early on, I thought that if I simply pointed out her mistakes and corrected her quickly, she would learn. But all it really taught her was to protect herself, to become defensive and to push me away when she needed guidance the most.

I learned, often the hard way, that reacting with quick punishments or long lectures only deepened the divide between us. It created fear, not growth. When a teenager feels attacked for messing up, they don't reflect; they retreat. They build emotional armour, not understanding. What they need most in those moments isn't a list of their failures, but a safe space to sit with what happened, a space where they are allowed to feel regret without being crushed by it. They need to be invited into reflection, not dragged into shame.

Now, when Kalpana messes up, I try to create that space intentionally. Instead of rushing to fix or correct her behaviour, I ask her questions designed to slow her down and help her think beyond the surface. I might ask, *"What part of that felt unfair to you?"* because often a poor decision comes from a deeper feeling of being misunderstood, sidelined or hurt. I ask, *"What do you wish you had done differently?"* not as a trick question, but as an invitation for her to reconnect with her better judgment.

When things are tense, I ask, *"What were you really feeling in that moment?"* because behind most anger there is something softer and more vulnerable; something that deserves attention. And when she seems stuck in self-defence, I ask, *"If the roles were reversed, how would you want someone to respond to you?"* to help her find her way back to empathy and self-compassion.

The point of these questions isn't to trap her into admitting fault or to soften the consequences of her actions. It's to guide her gently back to herself, to help her see her own story with more clarity and less fear. Reflection, handled with patience and kindness, teaches responsibility without creating shame. It helps her own her choices without making her feel like her mistakes define her worth. She begins to see that making a mistake isn't the end of her story; it's a moment in it and it can be a turning point if she is given the tools and trust to grow.

Helping her reflect isn't about letting her off the hook. It's about keeping her connected to her own heart even when she stumbles. It's about replacing the heavy burden of regret with the powerful gift of understanding. And it's about reminding her, again and again, that mistakes don't make her unworthy; they make her human. And being human is never something she has to be ashamed of.

When She Took Ownership

There are moments in parenting that feel like quiet victories; not because we win an argument or enforce a rule but because we see our child step into a new version of themselves. One evening, after days of silent treatment following a disagreement about phone rules, Kalpana surprised me. Without any prompting, without being cornered into apology, she came and stood beside me. Her voice was low, her eyes hesitant, but her words were clear:

"I think I overreacted."

In that simple sentence, I heard something bigger than an admission of guilt. I heard courage. I heard the beginnings of emotional maturity. It was the first time Kalpana had openly acknowledged her own role in a conflict without blaming, justifying or retreating. And it was tempting; deeply tempting; to seize the moment to prove a point, to say, *"See, I told you,"* to underline that I had been right all along. After all, how many times do we as parents long to be validated in the decisions we make for our children?

But I knew better. Growth, real growth, is fragile. It blooms not in the shadow of gloating, but in the warmth of grace. So, I swallowed the instinct to lecture, to preach, to make the moment about me. Instead, I simply smiled and said, *"It takes strength to admit that. I'm proud of you."*

And I meant every word. Because when a young person takes ownership of their behaviour, what they need most is not a reminder of their failure; they already feel it. They don't need an adult to rub it in, to magnify their mistake. What they need is someone who sees the courage it takes to be honest. Someone who encourages that tiny flicker of self-awareness into a steady flame.

In that small exchange, something shifted between us. Kalpana wasn't just apologizing; she was trusting me with her vulnerability. She was taking a risk; the risk of being honest, of owning her emotions without being punished for them. And because I met her honesty with respect instead of pride, that risk felt safe.

This is how real growth happens. Not in the moments where we prove ourselves right, but in the moments where we create space for our children to be wrong; and still feel valued. It happens when we show them that taking responsibility is not a trap, but a strength. That admitting fault is not a weakness, but a path toward becoming wiser, braver and more whole.

Rewriting, Together

Watching Kalpana grow has taught me that change isn't something that happens all at once. It's not marked by grand declarations or dramatic shifts. Instead, it happens quietly, almost invisibly, in the small choices she makes every day.

Every time she chooses kindness over ego; when she softens her voice instead of snapping back, when she holds space for someone else's feelings instead of rushing to defend her own; a tiny but powerful transformation takes place. It may not be loud or immediately obvious, but it matters. It's the beginning of a new way of being, one she is building with her own hands and heart.

It's the same each time she pauses before shouting. That brief moment that second of self-restraint before the explosion, is more than just her holding her tongue. It's her learning to respect her own emotions without letting them rule her. It's her discovering that strength is not always about speaking louder, but sometimes about listening deeper; even to herself. That pause, small as it seems, is a victory not just for the moment but for the person she is slowly becoming.

And when she apologizes; even in small, awkward, half-mumbled ways; it's another page in her story. Every time she says, *"I didn't mean to,"* or *"I shouldn't have done that," she* is practicing something that many adults still struggle with accountability with humility. She is learning that making mistakes does not make her weak, refusing to acknowledge them would. Every apology, however imperfect, adds to her capacity for courage, for connection, for self-respect.

Each of these moments may seem ordinary. On their own, they might pass unnoticed. But together, they are stitching a new narrative; one in which Kalpana owns her choices, honours her feelings and stays true to the values that matter most.

And as her mother, I am the quiet co-author of this story. I am not holding the pen for her. I am not writing the chapters. I am simply sitting beside her; sometimes cheering loudly, sometimes offering gentle edits, sometimes simply giving her the space she needs to wrestle with the words herself. I guide when I'm asked, support when I'm needed and trust her to find her voice even when the pages are messy or incomplete.

Because the goal isn't to write a perfect story for her. It's to give her the confidence and the freedom to write her own; with compassion, with resilience and with a deep, unwavering belief that she is the author of her life and she can always choose to begin again.

What I Hope She Learns

There are lessons I hope Kalpana carries with her long after these teenage years are behind her. Not lessons written down in a rulebook or shouted in moments of frustration, but lessons she quietly absorbs through the way we move through hard days together. Lessons planted not through lectures, but through love.

More than anything, I hope she learns that her past reactions do not define her. That the moments when she lost her temper, when she shut down, when she said things, she didn't mean; they are not the sum total of who she is. They are moments, not identities. Mistakes, not life sentences. I want her to understand, deep in her bones, that she is always bigger than her worst day.

I hope she comes to believe that she can always try again. That there is no such thing as being too late to choose differently. No mistake, no poor decision, no broken conversation can truly close the door to new beginnings; unless she decides to close it herself. And even then, she has the power to knock, to turn the handle, to walk back into growth whenever she is ready.

I want her to understand that she doesn't have to be perfect in order to be growing. Growth is messy. It looks like forward steps and backward ones. It looks like knowing better one day and struggling the next. It looks like being proud of yourself one minute and doubting yourself the next. Progress isn't clean or linear; and perfection isn't the goal. Being willing to keep going is.

More than anything, I want her to know that she is allowed; always allowed; to rewrite who she is, one page at a time. No label, no failure, no past reaction has the right to decide her future for her. She is the author of her story. She holds the pen. And each day, with each new choice, she has the power to add a new paragraph, a new chapter, a new ending.

One day, I know she will look back on this chapter of her life; the messy middle of growing up; and it will be tempting to focus only on the mistakes, the meltdowns, the things she wishes she had done differently. I hope, with everything in me, that instead she sees it for what it really is: a story of courage. A story of a girl who was brave enough to feel, brave enough to fall, brave enough to stand up again and keep writing.

Because growing up isn't about getting everything right. It's about learning how to hold your story with both hands; the messy parts and the beautiful parts; and saying, *"This is mine. And I'm proud of how I'm learning to live it."*

Chapter 15
She's Becoming Her, Not You

There comes a day; quiet, unspectacular and yet seismic; when you look at your daughter not across a school gate, not while lighting candles on her birthday cake, not while tucking her into bed, but across the vast and invisible space between who she once was and who she is now becoming. And in that ordinary moment, you realise something extraordinary: she's no longer looking at the world through your eyes. She's begun to see it through her own.

It doesn't happen all at once. There's no music, no ceremony, no clear beginning. Just a slow, almost imperceptible unfolding. A shift so delicate that if you're not paying close attention, you might miss it. One day, she no longer imitates the way you do your eyeliner; she critiques it. Another day, she voices an opinion you didn't ask for, tentative but firm, independent of yours. A shared joke you both used to love no longer makes her laugh; it makes her pause. And then comes the sentence you knew, someday, would come; but still weren't prepared for: *"I think differently now, Maa."*

And in that moment, something shifts inside you. It isn't exactly pain. It isn't exactly pride. It's a gravity you can't explain. A feeling that something is being set down, released, handed over. Not out of loss, but out of love. Not as a defeat, but as a quiet surrender. She is becoming herself. Not the version of her you once imagined, not a softer echo of you, not your little shadow updated with modern language and newer dreams. She is stepping into the world with her own shape, her own rhythm, her own angles, flaws, brilliance and vision.

And you, the mother, the first home, the first audience to her becoming; you are given a choice: Do you fight this evolution with subtle resistance, or do you rise to the occasion and witness it with awe?

I'll be honest; there were times I resisted it. Not with shouting or firm ultimatums, but in softer, more invisible ways.

But under every carefully worded concern, beneath every raised eyebrow I tried to disguise, was a simple, vulnerable truth: I was afraid. Not afraid of her dreams. Not even afraid of her failing. I was afraid of losing her. Afraid that as she walked further into her future, she would walk out of my reach. That as she grew into her world, she would no longer need mine.

That fear, I've come to understand, is deeply human; but also, deeply limiting. Because holding on too tightly to who our daughters used to be keeps us from seeing the breathtaking beauty of who they're becoming.

Kalpana is no longer the child who coloured neatly within the lines. She's the young woman now drawing her own lines; and sometimes scribbling through them halfway. Sometimes she colours outside the boundaries on purpose. Sometimes she rips the whole page up at 2 a.m. and starts over. My role is no longer to hand her the "right" colours. It's not to make sure her art looks like mine. It's simply to sit beside her, keep the light on and whisper in the midst of the mess, *"Go on. Keep going. I'm here."*

Letting go isn't detachment. It's a deep, mature kind of love. It's the quiet strength to protect the space where your child can sculpt herself, even when the shapes unsettle you

Somewhere along the way, in parenting a teenager, you realise that you're not the only one doing the shaping. You are being shaped, too. I've changed more in these past three years than I did in the thirty before them. I've learned to sit in discomfort without immediately reaching for control. I've learned to listen without needing to defend my own choices. I've learned to apologise without adding an explanation to protect my pride. I've learned to stay close while watching her hurt; and to resist the urge to fix everything just to ease my own helplessness.

I've learned to let her teach me things. To ask her what she needs, instead of assuming I know. To trust her instincts, even when they differ from mine. And above all, I've learned that love doesn't mean clinging. Love that clings become brittle. Love that holds loosely, that allows for movement, for mistakes, for transformation; that is the love that endures.

Kalpana is not mine to shape. She is not mine to control. She is mine to love; fiercely, unconditionally and with the kind of humility that knows she was never meant to become me. She was meant to become herself.

She once said something after a long conversation, almost in passing. But I haven't forgotten it. She said, ***"I don't want to become you, Maa. But I want to remember that you stayed beside me while I became me."***

I carry that sentence like a closing line to this chapter. A soft, steady reminder of what this journey is really about. Not **"She turned out exactly how I hoped."** But *"She turned out as she hoped; and I didn't stand in her way."*

That is motherhood, done with grace. That is love, lived with open hands. That is the joy of watching your child become someone you didn't plan for; but can't stop admiring.

So now, as Kalpana steps further into her life, I no longer grip her story in my hands. I simply cheer from the side. Not correcting. Not controlling. Just loving her, with a heart full of memory and eyes steady on her future.

And no matter where her path leads; even if it leads far from mine; I will still be here. A quiet light in the background. A soft place to return to. A voice that says, always and forever:

"Go ahead, my girl. You're not me.
You were never supposed to be.
You're you. And that's everything."

Acknowledgements

I extend my deepest gratitude to all the readers who have opened their hearts to this book. Your willingness to pause, reflect and journey through the complexities of motherhood and growing daughters alongside me is what gives this work its meaning. Thank you for your time, your empathy and your quiet encouragement — each one of you is part of the larger story this book hopes to tell.

A very special thanks to my daughter, who poured her creativity and care into formatting this book and designing its beautiful cover. Your talent, patience and understanding brought this work to life in ways I couldn't have imagined. This book carries my words but it holds your touch. I'm endlessly proud of you.